# MEASURING IMPACTS OF LAND DEVELOPMENT

## An Initial Approach

Philip S. Schaenman
Thomas Muller

The research and publication of this report were made possible through a research grant from the Office of Policy Development and Research of the U.S. Department of Housing and Urban Development under the provisions of Section 701(b) of the Housing Act of 1954, as amended, to The Urban Institute. The findings and conclusions presented in this report do not represent official policy of the Department of Housing and Urban Development or The Urban Institute.

THE URBAN INSTITUTE

*Library of Congress Catalog Card Number* 74-19854
ISBN 87766-214-1

U.I. 173-214-1

**REFER TO URI 86000 WHEN ORDERING**

C/76/3M

Available from:

Publications Office
The Urban Institute
2100 M Street, N.W.
Washington, D.C. 20037

*List Price: $2.95*



Printed in the United States of America

# FOREWORD

In many communities, poor land use decisions have given development and urban growth a bad name and a bad press. They have saddled many communities with unfortunate conditions which may take years to correct, if they can be corrected at all. It is not enough to decry the situation. A large body of opinion in both the private and the public sectors already agrees that "something should be done." Within the varied and, in many cases, restrictive legal, economic, and political framework in which land use policy must operate, there is an urgent need to devise better tools that can help local governments and others involved in the development process arrive at better land use decisions.

This report represents the early stages of one such tool or mechanism—a system for assessing the effects of land development proposals. No pretense is made that this system is yet a finished product, nor is it intended to encompass all the elements of sound land use planning and management. It is a rough beginning in one critical area. Its publication at this stage is intended to encourage elected officials, planners, developers, researchers and concerned citizens who are involved in land use matters to test at least parts of the system and to join in its further refinement.

The system presented here involves a comprehensive set of impact measures, and in the end still requires judgments of the findings. Unfortunately, there is no single litmus test or magic formula that yields a yes or no answer for all land use proposals. It is in the nature of land developments that almost every aspect of community life may be affected. One cannot assure sound land policy without considering the health of local business, employment opportunities, housing supply, local government services, transportation, crime, clean air and water, and all the other matters embraced in the set of impact measures. And even with the best impact estimates, officials must still weigh the likely outcomes of development in light of community goals. In the continuing work on this project, suggestions will be welcomed for ways to improve each aspect of the system to assure that the data collection techniques and analytic approaches for each measure are concise, to the point, reliable, economical, and practical for local governments.

An advisory group of elected officials, government planners, representatives of citizen's associations, and technical experts is helping to guide the overall work of this project. In addition, officials at the Department of Housing and Urban Development have contributed ideas to the project, and local government personnel are assisting generously in the continuing work on impact measures.

The Land Use Center was established by The Urban Institute in 1973 to focus on research, education, and technical assistance to various levels of government in the areas of land use and urban growth. The Center, under the direction of Worth Bateman, has several other studies under way describing the state of the art in impact measurement and analyzing the experience of selected state and local governments with it. These and other reports—concerned with land use governance, taxation, citizen participation, and regulatory policy—will be issued as the research is completed.

Washington, D.C.
November, 1974

WILLIAM GORHAM, *President*
*The Urban Institute*

# CONTENTS

**EXHIBITS**

# ACKNOWLEDGMENTS

The research supporting this work was sponsored by the Office of Policy Development and Research of the U.S. Department of Housing and Urban Development. The suggestions and encouragement of Wyndham Clarke, Director, Division of Community Planning, Development, and Conservation, and his deputy, James Hoben, have been greatly appreciated.

James Kalish and David Talbott, as consultants to The Urban Institute, and Dale Keyes, Kathy Christensen, and Grace Dawson of the Institute staff made important contributions to this report. Additional research assistance was provided by Nancy Tuck, Kathleen Hudak, and Peter Nelson. Walter Rybeck of The Urban Institute edited the overall report and contributed substantively to the content.

The study was initiated under the direction of Harry P. Hatry, Director of the State and Local Government Project of The Urban Institute. A second phase to further develop the proposed procedures is being continued under Worth Bateman, Director of The Urban Institute's Land Use Center.

The authors are grateful to Donald Fisk, Louis Blair, Michael Flax, John Hall, Damian Kulash, Frank deLeeuw, Henry Peskin, and Ralph Smith, all of The Urban Institute, for their useful critiques, and to Judy Fair and other members of the Institute's library staff for their help in support of the research.

Special thanks are also given to many individuals who critiqued an early working draft of this study and provided many valuable suggestions: Thomas Ragonetti, Cornell University; Jeffrey Luke, Planning Department, Scottsdale, Arizona; Professor Joseph Heikoff, State University of New York, Albany; Professor Rae Zimmerman, New York University; Norman Emerson, Office of the Mayor, and Nancy Minter and Hethie Parmesono, City Planning Department, Los Angeles, California; Sanford Getreu, former Planning Director, San Jose, California; Albert Gollin, Bureau of Social Science Research, Washington, D.C.; Robert Witherspoon and Sumner Myers, Institute of Public Administration; and Allen Schectel and Janice Levin, State Regional Planning Department, New Jersey.

The authors, of course, assume full responsibility for the present report.

P.S.S.
T.M.

# ADVISORY GROUP

The Advisory Group is assisting in the continuing efforts to improve the system described in this report for measuring the impacts of land development. As persons involved in the development process, they are providing a users' perspective to the work—that is, helping to assure that the suggested measurement procedures are practical and useful. This initial report, however, is the sole responsibility of the authors at The Urban Institute.

TIMOTHY A. BARROW / *Mayor, Phoenix, Arizona*

KURT W. BAUER / *Executive Director, Southeast Wisconsin Regional Planning Commission, Waukesha, Wisconsin*

FRANK H. BEAL / *Deputy Director for Research, American Society of Planning Officials, Chicago, Illinois*

MELVIN L. BERGHEIM / *Councilman, Alexandria, Virginia*

JOSEPH F. CATANIA / *Chairman, Board of Commissioners, Bucks County, Doylestown, Pennsylvania*

RICHARD F. COUNTS / *Zoning Administrator, Planning Department, Phoenix, Arizona*

CARL D. GOSLINE / *Director of General Planning, East Central Florida Regional Planning Council, Winter Park, Florida*

BERNARD D. GROSS / *Glover Park Citizens Association, and New Communities Program, HUD, Washington, D.C.*

HARRY P. HATRY / *Director, State and Local Government Research Program, The Urban Institute, Washington, D.C.*

TED KOLDERIE / *Executive Director, Citizens League, Minneapolis, Minnesota*

JACK LINVILLE, JR. / *Assistant Executive Director, American Institute of Planners, Washington, D.C.*

ALAN H. MAGAZINE / *Supervisor, Fairfax County Board, Fairfax, Virginia, and Project Director, Contract Research Center, International City Management Association, Washington, D.C.*

ROBERT H. PASLAY / *Planning Director, Planning Commission, Nashville, Tennessee*

RICHARD A. PERSICO / *Executive Director, Adirondack Park Agency, Ray Brook, New York*

JAMES R. REID / *Director, Office of Comprehensive Planning, Fairfax County, Virginia*

E. JACK SCHOOP / *Chief Planner, California Coastal Zone Conservation Commission, San Francisco, California*

DUANE L. SEARLES / *Special Counsel on Growth and Environment, National Association of Home Builders, Washington, D.C.*

PHILIP A. STEDFAST / *Planning Director, Department of City Planning, Norfolk, Virginia*

DAVID L. TALBOTT / *Director of Planning, Falls Church, Virginia*

RICHARD E. TUSTIAN / *Director of Planning, Maryland National Capital Parks and Planning Commission, Silver Spring, Maryland*

F. ROSS VOGELGESANG / *Director, Division of Planning and Zoning, Indianapolis, Indiana*

THORNTON K. WARE / *Planning Director, Rensselaer County, Troy, New York*

JOSEPH S. WHOLEY / *Chairman, Arlington County Board, Arlington, Virginia, and Director, Program Evaluation Studies, The Urban Institute, Washington, D.C.*

FRANKLIN C. WOOD / *Executive Director, Bucks County Planning Commission, Doylestown, Pennsylvania*

# SUMMARY

Local governments today face no more pressing issues than those surrounding land developments and rezonings within their jurisdictions. Is growth overruning the capacity of local facilities? Will new development pay its way or be a drain on present taxpayers? Intentionally or otherwise, are some segments of the population excluded from the benefits of new growth or made to bear disproportionate burdens of growth? For environmental or other reasons, should development be limited? Are local housing and employment needs being met?

The questions run on and on—and most of them are as tough to answer as they are important.

Elected local officials and planning commissions responsible for guiding or accomodating to urban change try to grapple with such questions but are severely handicapped by their limited time, staff, and money. Officials usually have to estimate the impacts of each development on an ad hoc basis, one at a time. The resultant evaluations often are not systematic or comprehensive. Estimates of intermediate outcomes are sometimes not translated into the likely end results for particular citizen groups and for the community as a whole. The evaluation dialogue among officials, developers, and citizens may raise vital concerns—"urban sprawl," "character of the neighborhood," "pollution," and so forth—but typically these are not adequately defined.

This report summarizes an initial attempt to outline an approach intended to help alleviate some of these problems. It sets forth measures and procedures for assessing the impact of land developments on economic, environmental, aesthetic, public and private service, housing, and social concerns. These measures and procedures are intended primarily to assist local decision makers and their staffs in confronting land use decisions in a more systematic way and with an emphasis on how citizens are affected. They also speak to the interests of concerned citizens and citizen groups by portraying potential impacts in a more understandable and open fashion.

The report concentrates on ways to develop comprehensive data on the expected impacts of development. This is viewed as only one of the vital elements in land use decision making. Other aspects, recognized as exceedingly important but only briefly mentioned here, include the overall planning process, administrative mechanisms needed to implement the use of impact measures, and the ways that communities—through the political system, citizen involvement, and the like—make the ultimate tradeoffs between alternative land use proposals.

Further development of the measures and data collection procedures are currently under way in cooperation with two local governments, and with the help of an advisory group of planners and elected officials from a wide variety of jurisdictions. Readers of this publication may participate in this effort to advance the state of the art of impact evaluation methods by considering this report a trial proposal to which their responses —queries, arguments, examples, and clarifications—will be most appreciated.

The use of impact measures will help clarify the likely advantages and disadvantages of a development, enabling officials and administrators to act more confidently to accept a proposal, to negotiate maximal positive aspects, to identify problems that require local policy changes, and to reject proposals when projections appear detrimental. In short, they should help communities better manage the course of future growth.

Some of the tentative recommendations emerging from the study to date follow.

## USE OF IMPACT MEASURES

1. *Local officials in each community should weigh each new development—residential, commercial, industrial, and public—against a check list of major considerations or impact measures.* Each community should develop its own check list based on local objectives. The measures should emphasize end impacts on citizens whenever possible. A suggested comprehensive list of impact measures that could be used as a starting point for various types of developments, and for evaluating existing as well as proposed developments is presented in Exhibit 1. The larger the development or the greater its potential impact, the more carefully each aspect of the check list needs to be considered. For most developments only a few measures are likely to be of sufficient importance to warrant detailed data collection. Systematic use of the check list approach for each development should help improve the consistency and comprehensiveness of evaluations, even if some of the measures can only be estimated crudely.

2. *Local officials can use most of the same list of measures for evaluating groups of developments and alternative comprehensive or sector plans.* Some measures are actually easier and likely to be more meaningful to consider for groups of developments or for overall growth than for individual small developments. This is especially so for the economic and some of the natural environment impacts.

3. *Land use impacts on specific clientele groups should be considered in addition to those for the community as a whole.* Various segments of the population, such as businessmen, residents of the neighborhood being redeveloped, or low-income families may be affected in quite different ways by the proposal. Some may be helped, some may be hurt, and others not affected significantly. Among the clientele groups to consider are those given in Exhibit 3.

4. *The impact of selected past developments should be evaluated regularly.* These evaluations will test the accuracy of impacts that were estimated—before those developments occurred—by both the local government and by the developer. The accumulated case histories will serve as a basis for improving future impact assessments for various types of developments. They may also aid in holding developers to their commitments.

## DATA COLLECTION AND PRESENTATION

5. *Data collection procedures relating to each measure on the check list should be specified and used consistently.* Part 2 of this report, while recognizing that the state of the art for many measures is rudimentary, offers a tentative description of such procedures. Some give fairly reliable results. At the other extreme are procedures still in the pretesting stage whose feasibility and practicality are uncertain.

6. *Procedures of different levels of detail should be developed for each measure to correspond to needs for both quick reviews and careful analyses.* Clearly, all developments cannot be evaluated in the same detail when large numbers of proposals are being presented to public bodies for decisions.

7. *The degree of uncertainty for each estimated impact should be explicitly stated.* For many land use decisions, highly precise estimates are not needed. However, the confidence in the estimate should be brought to the attention of policy makers and the public. In some instances it will be useful to give the range of possible impacts in addition to the "best" or "most likely" estimates.

8. *Impact measures should be displayed for decision makers in a readily understandable, nontechnical format.* Highlights should be presented in a few charts that summarize

impacts on various clientele groups and show the cumulative effects on groups of proposed developments. The degree to which the development fits in with the hierarchy of plans for the area, both in general and with respect to specifics, should also be indicated. Merely presenting vast quantities of technical data is not likely to improve decision making; the findings need to be distilled and translated.

## GENERAL ISSUES FOR LAND USE DECISION MAKING

9. *The collective impact of communitywide development activity should be considered in assessing any individual development.* The cumulative effects of all currently planned land use changes that have a reasonable chance of taking place—and not merely the isolated effects of each single development, which may appear quite insignificant—should be considered. The legal mechanisms surrounding land use decisions, however, are geared to separate actions on single developments rather than to policies affecting series and sets of proposals, so it will not be easy to maintain or act on the cumulative perspective.

10. *Spillover effects—the impact of land use decisions on neighboring jurisdictions—should be evaluated.* The political realities in areas where activities of adjacent communities are uncoordinated and highly competitive may make this goal difficult to achieve. If sheer altruism and concern for the larger public good will not generate action in this direction, perhaps self-interest will—that is, showing concern for neighbors may be a means of persuading them to reciprocate and give attention to spillover effects from their decisions. Because many localities have been indifferent to regional impacts, a movement is already underway to shift land use authority to regional and state governments; this movement is bound to gain momentum to the extent local governments continue to abdicate responsibility in this matter.

11. *Precedents require special attention.* Even when the immediate impact of a land use decision may be small, its long-term effects may be magnified if it involves new legal or policy directions. For example, allowing a small development in a previously protected woodland may have little immediate environmental, aesthetic, or recreational impact, but the pattern of encroachment could set off a chain of development with major effects.

12. *Alternative land uses and alternative sites—and not only those being proposed at a particular time—should be considered in the evaluation.* A community has a wide range of needs which may include low-income housing, moderate-income housing, employment, shopping, open space, and public facilities. Evaluations must consider the impacts of alternative ways that these needs may be met if the proposed development is not approved. Although the proposed development may have some negative impacts, they may not be as bad as some of the alternatives. Further development or deterioration of the site that may take place without any approval by the local government also should be considered, and not just the conditions that currently exist on the proposed development site.

13. *The check list approach of impact measures is not offered as a substitute for comprehensive analysis and reform of land use practices.* The approach described here is presented as a practical aid for local officials who do not have the luxury of waiting years or decades for ultimate, ideal solutions in deciding the development issues on their daily agendas, but who must decide on land use proposals one at a time. A growing number of observers believe that fundamental changes in land use theories, strategies, and policies are needed, based on detailed analyses of the operation of the real estate market, the influence of government programs and taxes on development patterns, and the labyrinth of present land use controls. Use of the measures in this report, while not aimed at that level of policy reconstruction, nevertheless may contribute to it by focusing public attention on issues in ways that suggest corrective actions.

# INTRODUCTION

With local governments and the general public increasingly concerned about changes in land use, and especially those involving higher intensity of use, the inadequacy of present tools for evaluating the impact of such changes has become apparent. A number of guidelines have evolved over the years—comprehensive plans, zoning ordinances, building codes, housing codes, subdivision regulations, and, more recently, state and federal requirements for environmental impact evaluations. These all have their strengths and uses, but they do not add up to a system that is sufficiently comprehensive in scope and specific in detail for gauging the effects of new developments. Officials and citizens alike are distressed at the mass of data but lack of useful information available to decision making.

It has become evident that improved techniques are needed for estimating the specific impacts of development on a community's economy, natural environment, public and private services, appearance, housing, and social conditions. This report suggests a set of measures and procedures that local governments may use for this purpose. It also offers a framework and a methodology for a community to arrive at its own set of evaluation criteria.

The report focuses primarily on ways to improve the evaluation of individual proposed developments—which, like it or not, is the most prevalent type of land use decision facing local and regional government officials. Many of the suggested measures also apply to evaluating cumulative effects of groups of proposed developments, and to evaluating alternative growth plans. For some measures, effects of individual developments are likely to be insignificant if viewed in isolation from other developments.

The same measures also may be applied to existing developments. Retrospective evaluations, although rarely undertaken by localities today, are strongly recommended for several reasons. They may identify consequences of earlier land use decisions that were not foreseen at all or that were incorrectly estimated at the time they were made, and thus throw light on how to make more reliable projections under similar situations in the future. Studies of past developments also may identify conditions that require corrective action by the developer or community.

This report does not deal more than incidentally with the way comprehensive planning determines and updates a hierarchy of local plans against which development should be evaluated. There is little discussion here about administrative mechanisms for implementing the impact measures set forth. And the report does not dwell in detail on how value judgments and tradeoffs about land uses are reached through the political process or meetings between officials, citizens, and developers. The importance of all these matters is recognized and they are being considered in the continuation of this study.

## CURRENT EVALUATION SHORTCOMINGS

Planners and others have called attention to many limitations and inadequacies of current efforts to evaluate proposed development. To note some of these briefly underscores the necessity for a new approach and indicates the kinds of gaps which must be bridged. Current evaluations are often characterized by the following features:

- A systematic, comprehensive approach toward identifying relevant criteria is often missing. Important social and economic considerations are often omitted altogether from the evaluation.

- There tends to be too much concern with technical criteria whose relationship to citizen or community well-being is unclear. Examples include floor area ratios

(FAR's), building setbacks, and persons per acre. One commentator on this situation has written that it is often assumed there is a series of links between controls and certain community goals when no such chain exists.[1] For instance, more restrictive FAR's will not necessarily reduce traffic congestion or a sense of crowding, nor assure privacy.

- The evaluation dialogue among planning officials, developers, and citizens is filled with generalities and with terms that are not well-defined, such as "urban sprawl," "character of the neighborhood," and "neighborhood stability."

- The evaluation criteria actually being used by the decision makers often are not openly stated and discussed. This may result from an attempt to avoid controversy, or simply because they have not had the time or staff to develop and document such criteria.

The measures and procedures offered in this report are intended to help alleviate the shortcomings just cited by providing a way to describe impacts on the citizens more explicitly, systematically, comprehensively, and in reasonably nontechnical terms. Any set of practical measures, however, is obviously unlikely to be satisfactory on all these scores. Nevertheless, there seems to be enough room for improvement within the resource limits of most governments to warrant the effort.

## AUDIENCE FOR THIS REPORT

The proposed measures and data collection methodology were devised primarily for municipal and county officials and their staffs who are involved in land use matters. It seems likely, however, that much the same approach would be useful to regional planning commissions, councils of governments, and state governments.

The emphasis on making the measures and procedures understandable also should give citizens more opportunity to participate constructively in land use matters.

## MANAGING A LARGE SET OF MEASURES

When faced with a rather large list of impact measures—forty-eight in all, as set forth in this report—local officials are likely to be concerned at first that this approach may be unwieldy and too expensive. It need not be.

It should be readily apparent that for any particular development, many of the impact measures will not apply. This is because the full list of measures is intended to apply to many types of development—commercial and residential, urban and suburban, large and small, existing and proposed. Measures that are not relevant to a particular development clearly may be bypassed. For most evaluations, the weeding out process will quickly lead to a relatively small subset of pertinent measures. Even among the latter, it is likely that only a few measures will assume major importance.

The proposed measurement procedures would indeed be impractical unless selectivity is exercised in both the choice of measures and the depth of analysis. In general, the more comprehensive and detailed analyses will be reserved for large developments, precedent-setting developments, and for sets of smaller developments whose cumulative effects appear to be significant.

As will be seen in the detailed discussion, two levels of data collection are discussed for some measures—one level for a brief, rough cut at estimating impacts (obviously the

---

1. Jacob B. Ukeles, *The Consequences of Municipal Zoning* Washington, D.C., Urban Land Institute, 1964.

more economical approach), and a second level where the community interest requires and justifies more thorough analysis. Most evaluations would use the simpler form, partly because of time, skill, and money constraints, but also because incremental impacts from individual developments are not likely to be substantial enough to justify voluminous data gathering and analysis.

## TERMS AND EMPHASES

*Land development.* As used in this report, land development refers to a significant change in the kind or intensity of use of a site. This includes, but is not limited to, land use changes that require rezoning.[2]

*Scale.* The scale of development to be evaluated may range from a single highrise structure to the reshaping of a major portion of a community.

*Private-public.* This report is oriented to development initiated by the private sector, although the measures presented here generally may be applied to the public sector as well. In the latter case, additional measures would be needed to determine the needs for constructing such facilities as hospitals and fire stations, and to more fully reflect their likely impact on service quality.

*Clientele groups.* The suggested measures are intended to reflect the concerns of citizens. All citizens, however, are not affected in the same way, or in the same degree, by particular developments. Therefore, besides looking at impacts on the community as a whole, it is advisable to estimate explicitly the impacts on different population segments. Unless this is done, the most articulate and aggressive groups may wield disproportionate influence to the detriment of others who have an equally legitimate stake in the community's future.

## ARE WE JUMPING THE GUN?

The authors recognize—and underscore the fact—that much of the work reported here is tentative and exploratory. It reflects only the initial phase of an ongoing study under HUD sponsorship to investigate ways to improve the methodology for evaluating land development. One school of thought is to withhold such material from public view until more definitive statements can be made.

However, because of the great interest in the subject today, it was decided to publish an initial report in the hope that the proposed measures and data collection procedures might provide a useful starting point for individual governments and stimulate them to improve their own evaluation methods. Second, it is believed that subjecting the work at this point to widespread review will be one important way of testing and advancing this approach in the shortest possible time.

## ORGANIZATION OF THE REPORT

The suggested measures and how they are formulated are presented in Chapter I of Part 1. Chapter II discusses the role of the measures—that is, how they may be used by local decision makers. Chapter III focuses on key methodological issues that have not been totally resolved but that should be kept in mind when applying the measures. Chapter IV indicates how the measures may be used to consider explicitly the impact of

---

2. A more detailed definition of land development is given in the proposed "Model Land Development Code," *American Law Institute*, 1970, pp. 8-11. (Unlike our definition, it excludes changes that can be made within existing zoning.)

development on different population segments or clientele groups. Chapter V suggests some ways of presenting or displaying the findings from the impact measures.

Part 2 deals with the more technical details of applying the proposed measures. It discusses the rationale, limitations, and alternative forms for each measure and outlines procedures for data collection in each instance.

# PART I: DEVELOPING AND USING A SET OF IMPACT MEASURES

*EXHIBIT 1*

## MEASURES FOR EVALUATING THE IMPACTS OF LAND DEVELOPMENTS

| Impact Area[1] | Measure |
|---|---|
| I. *Local Economy* | |
| Public Fiscal Balance | 1. Net change in government fiscal flow (revenues less operating expenditures and annualized capital expenditures). |
| Employment | 2. Number of new long-term and short-term jobs provided. |
| | 3. Change in numbers and percent employed, unemployed, and underemployed. |
| Wealth | 4. Change in land values. |
| II. *Natural Environment*[2] | |
| Air | 5. Change in level of air pollutants and number of people at risk or bothered by air pollution. |
| Water | 6. Change in level of water pollutants, change in tolerable types of use, and number of persons affected, for each body of water. |
| Noise | 7. Change in noise and vibration levels, and number of people bothered by excessive noise and vibration. |
| Greenery and Open Space | 8. Amount and percent change in greenery and open space. |
| Wildlife and Vegetation | 9. Number and types of endangered or rare species that will be threatened. |
| | 10. Change in abundance and diversity of wildlife and vegetation in the development and community. |
| Scarce Resource Consumption | 11. Change in frequency, duration, and magnitude of shortages of critically scarce resources, and the number of persons affected. |
| Natural Disasters | 12. Change in number of people and value of property endangered by flooding, earthquakes, landslides, mudslides, and other natural disasters. |
| III. *Aesthetics and Cultural Values*[3] | |
| Views | 13. Number of people whose views are blocked, degraded, or improved. |
| Attractiveness | 14. Visual attractiveness of the development as rated by citizens and "experts." |
| | 15. Percent of citizens who think the development improves or lessens the overall neighborhood attractiveness, pleasantness, and uniqueness.[4] |
| Landmarks | 16. Rarity and perceived importance of cultural, historic, or scientific landmarks to be lost or made inaccessible. |
| IV. *Public and Private Services* | |
| Drinking Water | 17. Change in rate of water shortage incidents. |
| | 18. Change in indexes of drinking water quality and safety. |
| Hospital Care | 19. Change in number of citizens who are beyond x minutes travel time from a hospital emergency room (using such time as the community considers reasonable). |
| | 20. Change in average number of days of waiting time for hospital admittance for elective surgery. |
| Crime Control | 21. Change in rate of crimes in existing community or new development (or expert rating of change in hazard). |
| | 22. Change in percent of people feeling a lack of security from crime. |
| Fire Protection | 23. Change in fire incidence rates. |
| | 24. Change in rating of fire spread and rescue hazards. |
| Recreation[5] | 25. Change in the number of people within—or beyond—a reasonable distance (x miles or y minutes) from recreational facilities, by type of facility. |
| | 26. Change in usage as a percent of capacity; waiting times; number of people turned away; facility space per resident; and citizen perceptions of crowdedness at recreational facilities. |
| | 27. Change in perceived pleasantness of recreational experience.[8] |
| Education[6] | 28. Change in number of students within x minutes walk or y minutes ride from school, by type of school. |
| | 29. Number and percent of students having to switch |

schools or busing status (from walking to busing or vice versa).

30. Change in crowdedness "breakpoints" (such as need for added shifts) or indicators (such as student-teacher ratios); student, teacher, and parent perceptions of crowdedness and pleasantness of schooling.

Local Transportation[7]

31. Change in vehicular travel times between selected origins and destinations.

32. Change in duration and severity of congestion.

33. Change in likelihood of finding a satisfactory parking space within x distance from destination or resident.

34. Change in numbers and percent of residents with access to public transit within x feet of their residences; and numbers and percent of employees who can get within x distance of work location by public transit.

35. Change in the rate of traffic accidents (or expert rating of change in hazard presented).

36. Number and percent of citizens perceiving a change in neighborhood traffic hazard; and change in pedestrian usage of streets, sidewalks, and other outdoor space.[8]

Shopping

37. Change in number of stores and services, by type, available within x distance of y people.

38. Change in the percent of people generally satisfied with local shopping conditions (access, variety, crowdedness).[8]

V. *Housing and Social Conditions*

Housing Adequacy

39. Change in number and percent of housing units that are substandard, and change in number and percent of people living in such units.

40. Change in number and percent of housing units by type (price or rent range, zoning category, owner-occupied and rental, etc.) relative to demand or to number of families in various income classes in the community.

People Displaced

41. Number of residents, or workers, displaced by development—and by whether they are satisfied with having to move.

Population Mix

42. Change in the population distribution by age, income, religion, racial or ethnic group, occupational class, and household type.

Crowdedness

43. Change in percent of people who perceive their neighborhood as too crowded.[8]

Sociability-Friendliness

44. Change in frequency of visits to friends among people in the existing neighborhood, and frequency of visits between people in the existing neighborhood and the new development.

45. Change in percent of people perceiving the neighborhood as friendly.[8]

Privacy

46. Number and percent of people with change in "visual" or "auditory" privacy.

47. Number and percent of people perceiving a loss of privacy.[8]

Overall Contentment with Neighborhood

48. Change in percent of people who perceive their community as a good place to live.[8]

Fairness to All Groups

The above measures should be considered with respect to specific clientele groups or population segments that are affected to reflect the quality of fairness in new developments.

**NOTES:**

1. These impact areas correspond to community objectives for regulating land development (see Exhibit 2).
2. In some situations, a measure of the change in the microclimate near a development should be added to the list.
3. Measures 5 through 10 also reflect aspects of aesthetics. See text for discussion of overlapping of objectives and interrelation of measures.
4. Some may find a new development physically attractive (Measure 14), but prefer the current appearance of the neighborhood for its "character," image, relation to personal identity, and so forth.
5. Changes in the use of informal recreational facilities such as streets, sidewalks, and open space should be included.
6. No satisfactory measure of development impacts on the quality of education received has been found.
7. Impacts of land use changes on accessibility by foot are reflected in part in measures for recreation (25), schools (28), and shopping (37).
8. Measures dealing with citizen perceptions are much harder to estimate quantitatively for proposed developments than for past developments. However, bounds or ranges may be estimated in some situations, and in all they should be considered at least qualitatively.

# I. SUGGESTED IMPACT MEASURES

To assess systematically the future consequences of proposed land development, each local government should have its own set of impact measures. The measures should be practical to implement and understandable to nontechnicians. The set of measures should be as short as possible yet comprehensive. Some communities may wish to prepare their set of measures "from scratch," based on their own local objectives. Others may prefer to use the list suggested in this report as a starting point, which they would review and modify to suit thier local purposes and values. In either case, it is necessary to understand not only what impact measures are, but how they are formulated.

## STARTING POINT—COMMUNITY OBJECTIVES

One logical way of arriving at a set of measures is to start with a list of major community objectives. The goals should be expressed as ends, not means, as targets, not strategies for reaching them.

Exhibit 2 presents an illustrative set of community objectives. The titles include the broad areas of communitywide concern that are or could be affected by patterns of growth and change. The statements accompanying each area of concern attempt to encapsule enlightened views of what should be achieved. In sum, they represent what those who frame the objectives consider to be the ideal community.

Generally, all objectives will not be advanced simultaneously by any single land development. As some objectives are being furthered, others may be affected adversely. This is one of the reasons that the basic list of objectives should be as broad as possible.

Realistically, the majority of people in a community at any given time tend to be most interested in only a few of their objectives—usually those about which problems or opportunities are being publicized and discussed. These few objectives are naturally accorded highest priority at the time. But if the system employed by planning officials requires reference to a comprehensive set of community goals, this should help guarantee that none of the other objectives will be completely ignored even though they may have low priority for a certain period.

## MEASURES TO MATCH OBJECTIVES

Once the objectives are determined and listed, they can be used as a starting point for defining appropriate impact measures. An essential feature of the impact measures is that they assist in evaluating the likely outcomes of proposed developments in terms of each community objective.

For example, maintaining the local government's fiscal solvency would be agreed upon in any community as a legitimate objective. An obvious measure for testing progress toward this objective is the estimated net fiscal change that will come about as a result of proposed developments. More specifically, this measure requires that, for any particular development, officials should estimate the difference between the additional local revenues which the new land use will generate and the public expenditures which it will require, as compared with the costs and revenues associated with the current land use.

Similarly, if a community objective is to maintain the present quality of local transportation, then measures might be chosen that will note changes in travel time, parking availability, and the accessibility of public transit.

Exhibit 1 on pages 10 and 11 shows the measures that have been identified for assessing the impacts of developments with respect to the community objectives previously outlined. Some objectives require more than one associated measure for an adequate assessment, and some measures are relevant to more than one objective.[1]

Local governments considering use of this list of measures might also scan the Appendix for "other measures" which, although judged less practical by the authors, may appear more suitable for their own local circumstances.

The measures delineated in Exhibit 1 can be utilized for evaluating sets of objectives other than those listed in Exhibit 2. For example, consider objectives cited in numerous rezoning cases: "preservation of the character of the neighborhood" and "retention of present life styles." While these objectives are rarely well-defined, the context of their use in suburban communities indicates that they frequently refer to such things as retaining the natural setting, avoiding crowdedness, maintaining a feeling of security, maintaining the present socioeconomic mix, and preventing traffic congestion. To assess the impact of new development from this perspective, the following measures in Exhibit 1 could be used: 7-8, 21-22, 25-27, 31-36, and 44-48. Likewise, those concerned with "maintenance of a safe and stable neighborhood" might refer to Measures 21-24 and 41-42.

In defining and selecting an entire set of measures, the attempt should be made to strike a balance between comprehensiveness and practicality. Therefore, the measures suggested do not cover every minute aspect of each community objective. Emphasis has been placed, rather, on important aspects most likely to be affected by development.

1. Measures sometimes apply to more than one objective when factors affecting the objectives overlap, as in the case of the objectives regarding aesthetics and preserving the natural environment.

## SELECTING MEASURES FOR EVALUATING PARTICULAR DEVELOPMENTS

For each development case under review, all measures should be quickly reviewed to determine whether they are appropriate. For few developments, however, will all measures need to be used.

More detailed and comprehensive analyses will in general be more appropriate for developments that are very large, for those that represent new departures in local growth patterns, for developments which could set important precedents, and for those which otherwise seem likely to have powerful short-range or long-range effects. Groups of developments likewise will tend to merit use of more measures and greater detail.

For smaller developments, some simpler alternative forms of the measures are discussed in Part 2 of this report. Many of the measures in Exhibit 1, nevertheless, can be used to evaluate smaller developments as well. Even when it is not appropriate to calculate everything quantitatively, some judgments may be reached.

During the initial screening, the appropriate subset of measures to use, and the level of analysis needed for each, will vary from case to case. Factors to consider in arriving at these subsets include the following:

### Type of Development

Some of the measures apply more to residential than to commercial developments. Some apply more to suburban than urban development.

### Local Conditions and Priorities

At the time land use decisions are being reached, local conditions will determine many of the measures that require detailed consideration. For example, measures of housing supply relative to housing needs that would be crucial in times of housing shortages could be only briefly considered and checked off when there is an adequate supply

*EXHIBIT 2*

## COMMUNITY OBJECTIVES FOR REGULATING LAND DEVELOPMENT[1]

**I. Local Economy:**

To keep the local government fiscally solvent without excessive taxes; to maintain a high level of stable employment and to reduce unemployment and under-employment in the community; to maintain prosperity; and to enable citizens in the community to achieve levels of personal income and wealth consistent with a decent standard of living (1-4).

**II. Natural Environment:**

To minimize pollution, protect wildlife and ecologically important features, preserve the natural environment, and conserve scarce resources (5-12).

**III. Aesthetic and Cultural Values:**

To protect and improve the physical and cultural attractiveness of the community (5-10, 13-16).

**IV. Public and Private Services:**

- *Health and Safety.* To minimize illness, injury, death rates, and property loss or damage (5-7, 17-24, 35-36, 39).
- *Recreation.* To provide a variety of accessible and enjoyable recreational facilities and programs in the community (6, 8, 25-27).
- *Education.* To provide quality education at all levels for all people in the community; to provide as diverse educational experiences as the community requires; and to assure the convenience and pleasantness of attending school (16, 28-30).
- *Local Transportation.* To provide access to an adequate choice of community services, facilities, and employment in a safe, quick, and convenient manner; and to move goods efficiently (31-36).
- *Shopping.* To promote the adequacy, variety, convenience and pleasantness of shopping for people in the community (37-38).

**V. Housing and Social Conditions:**

- *Housing.* To increase the opportunity for all citizens to obtain satisfactory housing at prices they can afford (39-40, 46-48).
- *Social Concerns and Community Morale.* To promote friendliness, psychological well-being, and good community morale while protecting individual's privacy and ability to regulate their interpersonal contacts (41-48).
- *Fairness to All Groups.* To apply each objective with equity to all within the community (1-48, reported by clientele group).

**NOTES:** 1. This set of objectives is illustrative. Each community should determine goals consistent with the desires and values of its citizens.

2. The numbers in parentheses following each objective correspond to the impact measures in Exhibit 1 which help describe whether a development will contribute to the objective.

3. The order of the objectives implies no ranking of priorities.

of satisfactory housing available for most income levels. Similarly, a community with abundant parks and open space easily accessible to all population centers would not need to emphasize recreation measures that would have high priority in cities with minimal outdoor recreation opportunities. However, even when conditions are obviously satisfactory, it might be good practice to note this in the summaries to let local decision makers know the issue was considered and judged to be no problem. This will tend to reinforce an awareness of, and a reliance on, the comprehensive approach and help assure that unexpected problems will not be overlooked in these areas at some future date.

### What Is Being Displaced?

In assessing development impacts, although there is a natural tendency to pay most attention to the proposed new use, the current land uses that would be displaced also need to be considered in weighing the consequences. In the case of downtown commercial buildings that will replace rundown housing, for example, the proposal should be assessed not only in terms of what would be constructed but also in terms of the number and price range of housing units demolished to make way for the development. Otherwise, the impact on the total housing stock of the neighborhood and city might not be evident.

### Interrelationships and Tradeoffs

The measures of impacts are often strongly related so it is important to consider them as a set. A change in one measure may affect others. Factors that at first may seem unimportant thus should not be too hastily discarded.

To illustrate, consider that for many new developments there is a tradeoff between government expenditures and the quality of public services. The tradeoff often varies with time. For example, certain facilities may be pushed to capacity by a new development before adequate relief can be afforded. Often, quality is allowed to slip in the interim. It is therefore necessary to discuss both the government expenditures and the quality of services, and how they will vary over time. Explicitly reporting both the fiscal balance and quality of services will help clarify the assumptions about service levels that went into the fiscal study, and may help ensure self-consistency among different parts of the evaluation. Similarly, when looking at other measures—changes in open space, housing, neighborhood appearance, and so forth—it is important to report all potential tradeoffs as explicitly as possible.

### Costs

In practice, the available resources—money, time, skills, and tools—often dictate the level of analysis as much as the factors cited above. Costs will vary widely depending on the size of the subset of measures used, the level of accuracy desired, the availability of suitable methodologies and data, the number of clientele groups for which distinct impacts need to be charted, the experience of the analytic staff, and the backlog of previous analyses that can provide useful comparisons. The expenditures for evaluations also should be in line with the size and importance of the developments to the community. Identification of the costs and skills needed for varying levels of analysis is on the agenda of research tasks in the continuation of this study.

## MAINTAINING PUBLIC SERVICES: CAPACITY MEASURES

A prime concern of officials is that new development will not so deplete the treasury or overload the capacity of current facilities as to cause local services to deteriorate. To reflect these concerns, we have suggested measures of both public fiscal balance and quality of services. In the course of developing estimates for these measures, it is usually necessary to consider how the capacities of various public facilities will vary over time as a result of development.

Capacity measures do not indicate direct impacts on citizens so it is preferable to translate them into those terms—such as the likely incidence of water shortages based on the capacity of water supply networks. But when this is too difficult or time consuming, the capacity data will serve as a useful surrogate. Even when the translation can be made, it might still be useful to provide data on capacities because they are operationally meaningful, provide another easily understood perspective on the impact of development, and will help provide reasonableness checks and insights into the estimations made for the main list of measures. Also, the capacity measures should be quite useful in assessing cumulative impacts of groups of proposed developments.

Capacity measures should be stated in terms of (1) the percentage of existing capacity utilized before the development, (2) the percentage of capacity to be utilized after development, and (3) the expected time until new capacity can be added to relieve any present or anticipated overload.[2] Capacities would be assessed for each facility likely to be impacted by the new land use, such as particular schools or particular sewage plants. Where specific facilities to be used by the development cannot be pinpointed, as is the case for facilities such as hospitals and sometimes parks, capacity would be assessed for groups of facilities. Where private utilities are likely to be affected by new development, the same kind of capacity measures may be applied. Examples and further discussion of how capacity measures may be presented are given in Chapter V.

---

2. The decision to add new capital facilities is sometimes beyond the direct control of local government, as is the case in most California jurisdictions where special districts for fire or parks, for example, are common. In addition, voter approval may be required. Thus distinction should be made between facilities already having passed such hurdles and almost sure to be built, and facilities which are more speculative. The latter should be listed as likely to be available no earlier than some specified date.

# II. HOW IMPACT MEASURES CAN ASSIST LOCAL DECISION MAKERS

The ultimate test of any set of impact measures is whether it can be used by mayors, city and county managers, city councils, county commissions, planners and planning boards, zoning boards, and other decision makers to arrive at better land use decisions for their communities.

## EVALUATING PROPOSED DEVELOPMENTS

The measures should be useful to officials by providing them with the means for evaluating what is seldom emphasized–the end results of development proposals from their constituents' perspective. Regular use of a set of measures for evaluation has the potential advantage over present approaches of being more comprehensive, of providing more quantitative information about key issues, of achieving more consistency by reference to the same framework and language, and of more clearly identifying who gains and who loses. The measures thus provide a systematic basis for helping public officials decide whether to accept or reject development proposals, to require modifications, or to choose among alternative proposals that are competing for the same resources.

Local officials are also well served by making the measures widely known throughout the community. Developers and architects, armed with knowledge of the evaluation criteria, are more likely to draw proposals that take account of basic community objectives. Concerned citizens also can more fairly and constructively monitor public action on land use matters if some of the mystery is removed from the evaluation process.

### Complementary to Existing Codes

The impact measures suggested in this report are intended to complement, not to replace, the use of applicable local, state, and federal codes that help ensure the physical safety and sanitary conditions of new building in most jurisdictions. These codes include zoning, building codes, subdivision regulations, health and sanitary codes, and fire and safety codes. Problems in safety and sanitation often arise through no fault of the codes but due to their inadequate enforcement. The measures provided in this report (Exhibit 1) do not duplicate these safety and sanitation considerations on the assumption that local codes will usually suffice in these areas.

### What Developments to Analyze

Governments usually will wish to use the measures to assess only significant developments (not trivial items such as single homes or backyard additions) and ones over which they have a reasonable degree of control. The most common situations of this sort involve proposed developments requiring zoning changes–rezoning, zoning variances, and special exceptions–as in the case of shopping centers and standard subdivisions.

Planned Unit Developments (PUDs), which attempt to accommodate higher population densities on parts of a site in order to provide more variety of open space and community amenities on other sections of the site, appear especially well suited to impact evaluations. This is because they are usually defined in more detail than other developments at the stage when rezoning is requested, making the analysis easier and more meaningful, and also because the local government typically may exercise more control over the specifics of PUD plans.

Impact analysis may be particularly useful in situations in which local government officials are authorized to award incentives or bonuses in exchange for features deemed to be in the public interest. In commercial areas, for instance, builders might be permitted to add one or two floors above the usual height limits in return for providing amenities for pedestrians.

Even if no regulatory tools are applicable, and no hazard is created by the development, a local government may still find it advantageous to evaluate a proposed development. The findings from such impact studies may be presented to the developer directly as a device for encouraging self regulation or they may be announced publicly to bring community pressures to bear.

For example, local officials might evaluate developments that seem likely to alter the community's revenue status and the pattern of demands for services plus those developments that may set other precedents regardless of which specific controls can be applied.

### Range of Development Options to Consider

In some situations, more than one development option for a particular site or several sites may be evaluated simultaneously. The impact evaluation must consider not just the potential changes from the existing baseline, but also the merits of the various options relative to each other.

In some jurisdictions, developers have considerable latitude to make major changes in their plans as originally proposed and approved, so long as these fall within a range of uses permitted within the new zoning category. An evaluation of future impacts in such communities should consider not only the proposed development, but also the broader range of potential uses to which the site may be put if the rezoning is granted.

Another dimension to consider is the impact of a proposed plan as compared with the impact if it is rejected. Presumably each development is intended to meet some demand. If not built, pressures are created to use existing facilities more intensely or to develop elsewhere. This can lead to increased housing prices, changes in migration patterns and so forth. Rejection of a proposed development also does not preclude changes in use of the existing site that do not require government approval. Thus the range of potential uses that are credible within the existing zoning should be considered.

While the complexities and high costs would limit the feasibility of carrying out comparisons of all such alternatives in detail, modest efforts in these directions will counteract the unrealistic notion that the alternative to a proposed land use is zero change in the community, or that the proposed development will not change considerably before it is constructed.

### Initial Screening

The advisability of a quick review of each proposed development against the entire check list of measures, referred to in the previous chapter, bears underscoring again. Local officials should conduct an initial screening of development proposals to determine whether they meet various codes and conform to community plans. If flagrant conflicts are found, no further examination is needed.

If a proposal passes this kind of test, a second screening of the impact measures will indicate areas that raise the most serious questions and that require detailed data gathering and analysis.

### When Quantification Is Weak

Does the measurement system fall apart and become useless in those cases when quantification is difficult or impossible? Not at all. Admittedly, there will be many instances when intensive data collection for certain measures is not feasible. Nevertheless, the specific consideration of each item on the checklist, even if it is only assessed qualtitatively, is likely to improve evaluations. For instance, simply to raise issues of aesthetics, privacy, or use of streets for informal recreation, even if the anticipated changes cannot be calculated with much precision, is more likely to set in motion the desired public and private improvements than if the matters were completely ignored during the approval stages.

### Weighing the Measurement Results

The system of impact measures proposed in this report is not a mechanistic approach; rather, it relies in the final analysis on judgments. The impact measures cannot be inserted into a formula that will give an automatic answer to whether a proposed land use change should be approved or disapproved. In particular situations, any one measure could become of great—or even primary—importance; yet the same measure may be insignificant in other times or circumstances. An a priori assignment of weights to each measure would therefore seem more likely to obscure than to clarify, and is not recommended. Instead, the findings must be considered by officials and concerned citizens in light of what they already know about the individual assets, needs, and political realities of their own community. In short, this system is intended to assist decision makers by giving them a way of obtaining improved information within an organized framework; they, not the system, must weigh the factors in each case.[1]

### Clientele Groups and Spillovers

One of the prevalent urban movements of this era is the persistent demand for equitable treatment. Neighborhoods, racial and ethnic groups, and persons of certain age categories often feel alienated because (justly or otherwise) they sense that they are receiving poor service or insufficient consideration by their government. Elected local officials and their staffs, even if highly motivated to meet this objective, may run afoul of it unless they have some way of keeping track of how different groups in their community are in fact treated. For this purpose as well as several others, the measures should be used to assess impacts of development in terms, not only of the city or county as a whole, but also for distinct segments of the population. This is considered of such current importance that a separate chapter—Chapter IV—is devoted to an elaboration of this point.

Spillovers—the impacts of development and land use decisions that affect neighboring jurisdictions or other parts of the metropolitan area—may be considered an extension of the concern for all clientele groups. These too are discussed further in the next chapters.

### Who Should Undertake Evaluations?

The responsibility for data collection and analysis may be assigned to local government staff, to contractors or consultants, or to responsible and broadly based citizen groups. Developers inevitably must be relied on for at least some of the data including design plans and projections for future use.

In any case, it is important that local government officials select or review the measures to be applied in a particular case and that data collection and analyses supplied by developers be carefully reviewed by the local government to maintain credibility of the results.

## EVALUATING PAST DEVELOPMENTS

The land use measures suggested in this report are designed for use in evaluating the actual impacts which have already occurred from previous developments as well as those likely to occur from the proposed developments. Retrospective evaluations by local governments of previously completed development have been rare, although they are beginning to be undertaken more frequently. They hold the promise of providing valuable feedback for those involved with impact evaluation. For example, they might be used for the following purposes:

- To compare actual impacts with what the developer estimated or claimed when the proposal was made. As confidence is

1. An excellent, detailed discussion of the tradeoff problem and of various formal approaches for making a decision in light of incommensurable data may be found in Douglas C. Dacy, Robert E. Kuenne, and Martin C. McGuire, *Approaches to the Treatment of Incommensurables in Cost-Benefit Analysis:* Prepared for the National Science Foundation by the Institute for Defense Analysis, Program Analysis Division, Arlington, Virginia, 1973.

gained in the measurement procedures, the comparisons might even become a basis for rewards or penalties to developers. Those who comply with or exceed their promised landscaping or parking arrangements, for example, may become eligible for performance bonuses. Those who do not comply might be penalized or held to more concrete assurances in their future developments. The intent would be to improve the quality of predevelopment estimates by the developers and to encourage their continuing interest in their projects (in contrast to a "hit-and-run" attitude).

- To monitor the quality of the local government's decision making, again by comparing actual impacts with those predicted. Of course, many factors change over time, so the fact that different results occur than were predicted—either by developers or officials—does not mean that the original decision was necessarily inappropriate.

- To use the past to help predict the future. As a community completes studies of different types of previous developments, the findings will provide a series of case histories that, if carefully used, can help indicate the most likely impacts when similar plans and circumstances are going to reoccur. Often, reasonable quantitative projections cannot be made except by this kind of analogy to past experience, as in trying to assess citizen perceptions of crowdedness or neighborhood pleasantness. Retrospective evaluations would be even more useful if they were generated by groups of similar communities so that a broader data base could be generated. A cooperative venture of this sort might be undertaken under the auspices of municipal, county, or state professional associations.

- To give greater insight into direct and synergistic effects of development. One may project the individual elements of a proposed development with some accuracy but still fail to predict some of the overall effects that will come to light only after it is completed.

Full retrospective analyses can be expensive so local jurisdictions must be highly selective in undertaking them. But their high potential for revealing insights on the effects of development should not be ignored.

Certain obvious differences will occur in applying the measures to future and past development. For past developments, data collection and analysis can focus more on measurements of actual changes than on estimates, although there is often a problem of attributing changes to the development rather than to other factors. Assessments of future developments, however, must rely more on estimations. The direct measures that can be used for tracking impacts of past developments must sometimes give way to proxy measures when efforts turn to forecasting. For example, wildlife surveys made before and after development can help indicate the change in wildlife abundance due to past development. However, forecasting changes in wildlife due to proposed development may often be too complex, and a proxy such as the change in available acreage of habitat may have to be used instead. Building a repertory of retrospective evaluations should help local governments estimate end effects rather than proxies.

## EVALUATING COMPREHENSIVE AND NEIGHBORHOOD PLANS

The use of impact measures to assess specific developments is the main thrust of this report, but the measures proposed here also may be used—with minor variations—to help evaluate comprehensive plans, neighborhood plans, and other area plans.[2] This application of the measures to land use plans is even more suitable in some respects than to individual developments. More resources can be

2. One example of the use of a set of measures for evaluating comprehensive plans is described in the Southeastern Wisconsin Regional Planning Commission, Report No. 7, Volume 2, circa 1963.

devoted to the task and some of the techniques lend themselves more readily to detecting large-scale impacts.

Applying a full impact analysis to general plans, however, is not without its difficulties. Such a wide range of developments usually can occur within the limits defined by a given plan that a large number of alternative projections have to be made and the degree of uncertainty may be considerable. Although bounds can be developed for many measures, they may of necessity be fairly gross. Comprehensive plans are usually made to last for several years, yet long-range estimates may be invalidated by changes in technology (e.g., vehicular pollution controls), the emergence of new problems (e.g., the energy crisis), or altered mores and values within the community. Despite these problems, the use of impact measures within this context nevertheless appears worthwhile.

Local governments, going further, may find that they can strengthen their comprehensive land use plans by imbedding within them quantitative targets or constraints related to many of the impact measures. If this were done it would provide an excellent yardstick for evaluating individual and cumulative effects of proposed developments. Much baseline data useful for evaluating individual developments, such as natural resource inventories and maps showing the existence, capacities, and extent of utilization of public facilities, can be generated in the process of creating and updating comprehensive plans.

# III. PUTTING THE MEASURES IN PERSPECTIVE

To avoid an overly simplistic view of the impact measures and their application to land use decisions, several complex but important issues need to be stressed. Some of these have been touched on in earlier chapters and are explained more fully here. The discussion that follows, nevertheless, still only skims the surface, but aims to raise certain caution signals. The issues fall into two broad categories:

- Relating the estimated impacts of specific developments to the community and region at large, taking account of the collective effects of series of developments over time.

- Paying attention to hard-to-evaluate institutional, procedural, and political problems, some of which may be caused by the introduction of an explicit, well-defined set of impact measures itself.

## RELATING IMPACTS TO THE COMMUNITY AND REGION AT LARGE

### Collective Effects of Development

Many impacts of a specific development or set of developments often can be assessed realistically only with the context of (1) cumulative impacts of past developments, such as the current air quality and public perception of community conditions, (2) potential impacts resulting from changes in the use of present structures and facilities, as when a maturing community with a declining birth rate demands fewer classrooms, and (3) future land use changes that are likely to occur in the community, including other proposed developments. This context is especially important for local officials to keep in mind when they are making separate decisions on each request for land use change.

The collective impacts are important for several reasons. First, individual development decisions often combine in complex ways. Their total impacts, in respect to many social, economic, public service, aesthetic, and environmental measures, are not simply additive, but may amount to something more than and different from the sum of their parts. Extensive development may lead to fundamental changes in the community. For example, a semi-rural community on the perimeter of a metropolitan area often can maintain its small town character with the addition of a few small residential or commercial projects. But at some point in the growth cycle as more and larger developments occur, the character of the population and its demands for public services may change substantially, requiring changes in the structure of public services. For instance, a volunteer fire department may give way to a fulltime professional one. Or the number of police per capita and their form of organization may change, not just because crime rates often increase as communities grow, but also because of new demands for services such as traffic control. Considerable evidence indicates that the unit costs of public service change as a jurisdiction's size and population density increase. In short, the whole tenor of community life may be transformed.

These kinds of change, however, are not usually attributable solely to single developments unless they are large relative to the existing community. For this reason, the application of impact measures to individual developments needs to be viewed within the context of an area's total urban growth process lest the forest be lost for the trees.

A second major reason for considering collective effects of developments is that the impacts of a single land use change on some important community characteristics is often inconsequential. For example, the contribution to air pollution of 200 new units of housing, though measurable, is likely to be quite small. In some situations even small changes could be important—as when the pollution level is already approaching or exceeding some definable critical point. More commonly, however, it would be necessary to evaluate not only the 200 new houses but the entire group of proposed or anticipated developments over the next year or so for their collective impact on air quality. The assessment, of course, should also take into account any likely changes in existing community activities or regulations that may affect emissions, such as increases or decreases in car trips per person, new pollution controls on cars, changes in public incineration, and so forth.

A third major reason for considering collective impacts is that some proposed developments might counteract the positive or negative effects of other proposed developments. For example, an urban renewal project that proposes a park for small children could receive high grades on that account. But another development proposed in the vicinity of that park might make traffic so hazardous as to render the park inaccessible to small children. Unless both projects were considered together, unrealistic and unreliable forecasts would be obtained.

### Spillover Effects

Many large developments have significant environmental and economic effects beyond the boundaries of their immediate jurisdiction. Examples are water pollutants dispersed through a drainage network, or air pollutants emitted into an air shed—they seldom disappear neatly at political boundaries. Likewise, industrial and commercial developments typically draw labor force and consumers from beyond the municipality where they are located, which may produce favorable or unfavorable consequences for their communities.

Many of the measures listed in Exhibit 1 could apply to regional as well as local impacts. However, the regional effects of individual developments are often too diffuse to isolate. Thus, even more so than at the community level, the collective impacts of regional development need to be considered for a proper perspective of spillovers and counterbalancing spill-ins.

Unfortunately, a governmental agency for assessing greater-than-local development impacts often does not exist. Local governments have little incentive other than a sense of fair play, and a hope that their neighbors will reciprocate, to spend the effort—and it is likely to be considerable—in examining spillover effects beyond their borders. Councils of governments, regional councils, and some units of state government are starting to fill this void for some classes of development. But institutional and political barriers that discourage cooperation among neighboring communities and the technical difficulties of gathering and analyzing data on metropolitan-wide impacts still pose major hurdles to adequate consideration of spillover effects.

### Secondary Impacts

New developments frequently induce additional economic activity. Industrial and commercial growth often attract inmigration which translates into demand for new housing and shopping centers. These demands stimulate additional construction, both private and public. All these activities have environmental, social, and economic impacts.

Local government has some subsequent control over these ripple effects or secondary impacts. For example, officials have the alternative of disapproving land use change requests that are stimulated by previously approved developments. However, such refusals themselves can have secondary effects. In the case of industrial development, suppose that requests to rezone land for housing to meet residential demands generated by the new industry are denied. This would tend to cause prices of existing housing to rise. Some families, particularly those in the lower income range who could no longer afford the higher housing costs, may be forced to leave the community. This could cause a drop in school attendance or in the demand for other public services, and a whole chain of effects in the public and commercial sectors.

Although the significance of secondary effects of development has long been recognized, forecasting and measuring these effects with any precision still appears to be beyond present capabilities. Analysts have attempted to incorporate projections of secondary effects in urban computer modeling without a great deal of success. Yet it seems desirable, as part of land use impact measures, to do one's best to anticipate the possible kinds of secondary impacts that may occur and to estimate them at least qualitatively, and to note the directions and orders of magnitude of the impacts where feasible. When such an exercise suggests that the secondary effects will be substantial, this information should be included along with the direct measurement data presented to the decision makers.

## INSTITUTIONAL, PROCEDURAL, AND POLITICAL ISSUES

### Precedents

A land use decision which sets precedents for the future may assume an importance far greater than would be implied by any immediate impacts of the specific development as reflected by the measurement data. Once an approval of this kind is made, it can be extremely difficult to reject proposals for similar developments. The builder may appeal not only to logic—that he is following suit in a pattern already endorsed by the authorities—but also to the law, claiming that equal treatment provisions support his right to do what another developer was allowed to do.

A number of potentially precedent-setting situations often involve development of a previously untouched area or a major change in the intensity of development:

- The first residential subdivision in a farmland area.
- The first highrise in a single-family home neighborhood.
- The first development on a strip of virgin beach.
- The first construction in a forested area.

Another type of precedent, often a result of one of the above, is the first major deviation from the existing comprehensive plan. This may lead to further deviations, which could accelerate the erosion of the plan. This may not necessarily be detrimental, but as a possible long-term effect of the land use decision at hand, such an important direction should be taken deliberately, not merely entered into by default.

A totally different type of precedent would be the adoption by a city or county of a new standard for evaluating land use questions, as would be the case the first time that impact measures comparable to those proposed in this report were revealed to the community and put to use. Once the explicitly stated new measures are used to evaluate a development, it may be difficult to change or abandon them in future cases without the government being subjected to charges of unequal treatment or capriciousness. So a community should exercise care to choose a set of measures that is likely to be stable for some time.

### Political Problems

At least one potential political problem that may arise from the application of land use impact measures needs to be highlighted: their use could increase community conflicts, at least in the short run. This is because explicit, quantitative data may bring to light problems and inequities that were previously unknown, unmentioned, or only vaguely sensed. This is especially likely when impacts on various clientele groups are reported.

For example, the data may spotlight a public fiscal loss associated with a proposal for low-income housing or the negative environmental impacts from a new job-creating industry. Decision makers who strongly favor the improvement of housing and job opportunities may consider it undesirable and contrary to the community's best interests to publicize information that could arm the opponents of low-income housing and industrial growth.

On the other hand, making the evaluation more explicit, quantitative, and comprehensive may help lay some community fears and myths to rest. For instance, concerns about increased traffic or pollution might be allayed if the degree of anticipated increases were spelled out. In the long run, a more open and intelligible decision making process should improve the quality of decision making. Equally important, such an open policy should help restore confidence in government—the lack of which is certainly one of the more serious ills of current American society.

### Information Overload and Aura of Precision

The use of a large set of impact measures has the potential danger of overwhelming or bewildering decision makers with information about more aspects than they can grasp. Fears also have been expressed that masses of statistical information might convey to officials and citizens a misleading appearance of precision so that undue reliance would be placed on the estimated impacts. These dangers, while real, are common even to current procedures and to most management information systems. To be alert to the dangers is the first step toward minimizing them.

The comprehensiveness and depth of analysis that can be absorbed by decision makers depend on several factors—the care taken in developing data formats that can be quickly understood; the degree to which technical data are translated into meaningful descriptions of future impacts on citizens; and the attention given to educating local officials about data collection procedures and the measures that will be regularly presented to them. These factors may be as critical as the improvement of data gathering and analytic techniques.

### Delays and Costs in Decision Making

The work of collecting data for the proposed measures and setting up new procedures is likely to require additional governmental staff time and resources, at least initially. It might also increase costs to the developer because of increased data requirements levied on him or from additional delays in arriving at a decision on his proposals. These costs may be passed on to consumers. Systematizing and documenting the impact evaluation process, however, might conceivably result in lower overall analysis costs and time—that is, the sum of developer, public sector, and private citizen costs. Each evaluation, for instance, would be somewhat less of a special study with its own models, tools, and approaches than is the case today. The proposed system offers the potential for creating computer models and survey instruments that, once in existence, could be applied to many development decisions. These analytic tools also may be offered by local government to developers, consultants, and other private interests for their own purposes, possibly on a fee-for-service basis.

But the main reason for using a more systematic approach is to improve the quality of land use decisions. That is where the largest potential savings to the public lie. Without having some belief that this will be the result, it would be hard to justify adoption of the system on cost arguments alone.

* * *

On balance the risks involved in using the measures and the inability to resolve adequately all the issues discussed above seem less serious than the problems associated with failure to move ahead on improvements of the current land use decision process. Each local jurisdiction obviously must consider the many tradeoffs from its own vantage point.

A point which would not have had to be made until recent years is that a good deal of the discussion in this report about the complexity of growth should not necessarily be interpreted as arguments against community changes. Many citizens and interest groups, frustrated by the shortcomings and disappointments of current land use practices, are indeed taking this position. The point of this report is not so extreme or absolute. Rather it holds that the options for change should be examined more carefully and systematically, and selected with more discrimination than often has been the case.

# IV. CLIENTELE GROUPS

The impacts of development do not fall evenly across a community. As a result of changes in land use, benefits are enjoyed and losses are suffered in various ways and to various degrees by many different groups—such as the owners of the development site, nearby residents, commercial interests, and persons being displaced.

When development proposals are being reviewed by officials, some of the affected groups and individuals present arguments pro and con. These persons who have the time, awareness, know-how, and economic wherewithal to come forward may not represent all of the numerous groups having an important stake in the decisions. For example, low-income families and residents or small businesses just beyond the immediate neighborhood of the development site often do not have advocates at the hearings to represent their views and interests.

Evaluations of development, therefore, should not be limited to estimating communitywide impacts. They should also attempt to identify significant impacts on distinct clientele groups within the community, and preferably on groups outside the community as well.

Identifying impacts on various clientele groups should help clarify how the beneficial and detrimental effects of development are distributed and prevent a positive effect on one group from being offset by a negative impact on another. The negative impact may not be noticed if the impacts are reported as an average across all groups. This approach also may help officials to identify aspects of proposals which require modification before plans should be approved. Over the long run, it should help indicate when the burdens posed by development, instead of being shared uniformly, are being borne to too large an extent by particular groups. Impact analysis by clientele groups might also serve to further the dialogue between decision makers and citizens although, as noted in the previous chapter, explicitness may carry its own set of potential difficulties.[1]

For various land use proposals, different sets of clientele groups need to be considered. The pertinent groups depend on the type, size, and location of the development. The clientele groups that follow in outline form (see also Exhibit 3) are merely suggestive or illustrative of the ones that may be appropriate in any given situation. The clientele groups are described briefly. Some of the issues that merit consideration for these groups are listed; in most cases the link between these issues and the impact measures discussed earlier should be obvious. The assessments from the perspective of clientele groups will be more valuable to officials if the size of each group for which impacts

---

1. The mechanisms for increasing public involvement in land use planning, with particular attention to the balancing of active interest groups, affected interest groups, and the general public, have been studied by Nelson M. Rosenbaum of The Urban Institute. See Nelson M. Rosenbaum, "Citizen Involvement in Land Use Governance: Issues and Methods," Working Paper 0785-04. The Urban Institute, Washington, D.C., July 1974.

*EXHIBIT 3*

## CLIENTELE GROUPS POTENTIALLY AFFECTED BY DEVELOPMENT

**Physical Proximity**

Persons living or working on the land proposed for development

Persons living or working immediately adjacent to proposed development

Persons in neighborhoods surrounding the proposed development

Persons within commuting distance (one hour by public transit, for example) from proposed commercial and industrial developments

**Business Relationship**

Builders, realtors, bankers, and others directly involved in the development

Owners and managers of businesses or property in the neighborhood

**Political Jurisdiction**

Citizens of local jurisdiction containing the development

Citizens of immediately adjacent jurisdictions and of entire metropolitan area

Citizens of the state and nation

**Socioeconomic and Demographic**

Age groups

Racial and ethnic groups

Persons of various income levels, from poor to affluent

**Other Interest Groups**

Tourists

Land owners

Others

**The Long-Term Public Interest**

All present groupings over time

Future generations

**NOTE:** This list of population segments that merit consideration is illustrative and is not all-inclusive for every situation. Many other categories will be readily apparent within the context of specific impact measures. For example, in considering transportation impacts, an important distinction to make is between persons and families with and without automobiles.

are reported is indicated in summary charts for decision makers, as illustrated in the next chapter.

The groupings listed are not formal organizations, associations, lobby groups, or the like. Rather, they are categories of people or interest groups that are likely to be affected in different ways by development.

## A. GROUPINGS BY PHYSICAL PROXIMITY TO THE DEVELOPMENT

1. Persons currently living or working on land to be developed.

   Issues: Availability, accessibility, quality, and cost of relocation housing. Earnings at new jobs. Disruption of social ties. Changing schools for children. Relative satisfaction with the neighborhood in likely new locations.

2. Persons living or working on land adjacent to the development.

   Issues: Almost all measures (Exhibit 1) are relevant for this group.

3. Persons living or working in neighborhoods around or near the development.

   Issues: Most measures are relevant for neighborhoods—which may be defined by well-mapped boundaries (as in the case of neighborhood service areas), by socioeconomic characteristics of residents, or by proximity to the development, such as "10 minutes walking distance." Traffic, crime, air and water pollution, and crowding of major recreation facilities are among effects that may spill over into several neighborhoods. Impacts on noise, views, sociability, and privacy tend to be more localized (but this should be checked against the size and design of the specific proposal).

4. Persons within commuting distance or usage range of the development.

   Issues: Those in this group vary according to the type of development. For a work center, the people included are those within the locally acceptable commuting distance or time—for example, one hour by public or private transportation. For a regional shopping center or amusement park, the people may include those in a much larger area. Note that the number of people within commuting distance cannot fairly be assessed until the effects of the development itself on public transit service, new roads, and traffic congestion are estimated. Note also that the area under discussion may include most or all of a metropolitan area and, in some instances, multistate areas. Among the many relevant measures for commercial or industrial developments are changes in employment, recreation, shopping availability, travel times, and pollution along commuter corridors. Residential developments need to be assessed in terms of available housing relative to job locations.

## B. GROUPINGS BY BUSINESS RELATIONSHIPS TO THE DEVELOPMENTS

1. Businessmen directly involved in the development, such as builders, realtors, and bankers.

   Issues: Businessmen may be concerned with a wide range of economic, social, and environmental changes that will affect the profitability and safety of their investment and their reputation in the community. Most impact measures, not simply the economic ones, are of interest.

2. Owners and managers of businesses or property in the neighborhood.

   Issues: Number and mix of potential customers, new business competition, public safety, property values, quality of public services, and environmental impacts.

## C. GROUPINGS BY POLITICAL JURISDICTIONS AFFECTED BY THE DEVELOPMENT

1. Citizens of the local jurisdiction.

   Issues: Changes in taxes, community fiscal solvency, local economy, employment, public service quality, crime, natural environment, and so forth.

2. Citizens of nearby local jurisdictions and/or of the entire metropolitan area.

   Issues: Basically the same impacts affecting the jurisdiction where the development will occur also need to be considered for possible spillover effects, of which economic, pollution, housing, and transportation impacts are often among the most important.

3. Citizens of the state.

   Issues: State taxes and revenues. State public services. Regional environmental changes. Statewide employment and housing patterns. Attractiveness of state's industrial climate. Important state landmarks or scenic attractions. Energy consumption.

4. Citizens of the nation.

   Issues: Federal taxes and outlays. Multiregional pollution. Overall housing and employment opportunities. Impacts on minority and low-income groups. Preservation of national landmarks. Scarce resources. Cumulative effects and development trends will generally be of more concern nationally than will the impacts of single developments. Innovative features of the development, of the zoning, of the decision making process, and of criteria used–and court opinions on any of these aspects–are of widespread interest.

## D. GROUPINGS BY SOCIOECONOMIC AND DEMOGRAPHIC CHARACTERISTICS

1. Age groups, such as children and the elderly.

   Issues: Education, traffic safety, recreation for children. Public transit, housing, noise and pollution, health hazards, neighborhood social conditions, recreation, and crime protection for the elderly.

2. Ethnic, racial, and religious groups.

   Issues: Equal opportunities for housing, education, recreation, and employment. Neighborhood social composition.

3. Income groups.

   Issues: Housing and employment opportunities.

## E. OTHER INTEREST GROUPS

1. Tourists.

   Issues: Landmarks, scenery, shopping, public safety.

2. Land owners.

   Issues: People who own property, whether for use or for investment, have a special interest in the local economy, the tax climate, and the cumulative land use impacts.

3. Distant viewers of the development.

   Issues: People at some distance from a development site (across the river or on a mountain overlooking a valley) should be considered if the changed land use will block their view or create (or remove) an eyesore.

## F. THE LONG-TERM PUBLIC INTEREST

Issues: Considering this group focuses attention on future generations and on all groupings over time. Enduring impacts on the physical environment, waste of natural resources, tax trends, pollution, wildlife, landmarks, and aesthetics all assume greater importance from this perspective.

Most of what has been said about the use of impact measures in general applies to the measures when they are seen from the perspective of clientele groups. These interest groups should be used first as a check list for a quick screening so that none are forgotten. Time and money may be conserved in evaluations by narrowing this list to smaller subsets of clientele groups likely to be affected most significantly before launching into more detailed analyses.

*EXHIBIT 4*

## ILLUSTRATIVE DISPLAY OF IMPACT MEASURE DATA

Hypothetical Proposal: 20-story office building with shopping plaza replacing tenement housing

| IMPACT AREA | MEASURE[1] | IMPACT ON CLIENTELE GROUPS[2] | | | COMPLIANCE WITH COMPREHENSIVE PLANS |
|---|---|---|---|---|---|
| | | A. Local Jurisdiction (50,000 people) | B. Immediate Neighborhood (500 people) | C. Low-Income Families in the Jurisdiction (5,000 people) | |
| Local Economy | (1) Change in net fiscal flow | + $200,000 to $300,000 | N/A[3] | N/A | N/A |
| | (4) Net number of new jobs | +200 to 300 jobs | +10 to 20 jobs | +50 to 70 jobs | Yes |
| Aesthetics | (15) Number of people whose views will be blocked | 300 to 400 people | 250 to 300 people | 250 to 300 people | N/A |
| | (16) Percent people (in random survey) finding development attractive | 75% (of sample) | 40% (of sample) | N/A | Partly Yes, Partly No. (General opinion is in compliance, local opinion is not.) |
| Air Pollution | (7) Number of additional people expected to be exposed to x p.p.m. for over y hours more than z times a year | +4000 to 8000 people | + 300 to 500 people | N/A | No |
| Local Transportation | (37) Change in average auto travel time to reach destination x in neighborhood | +3 to 5 min. | +3 to 5 min. | N/A | No |
| Housing Stock | (42) Change in number of housing | -50 substandard units | -50 substandard units | -50 substandard units | Partly Yes (removal of substandard housing) Partly No (accommodations for displaced families) |
| Neighborhood Stability | (48) Number of residents displaced | 150 | 150 | 130 | Yes |

1. Numbers in parentheses refer to measures in Exhibit 1.

2. See Chapter IV for a discussion of clientele group interests. These are illustrative of only a few clientele groups; others would also be pertinent. Note that some of the same people may be in groups A, B, and C.

3. An estimate of whether the remaining families in the neighborhood will pay more or less property taxes due to changes in property value might be given here.

# V. DATA PRESENTATION FORMATS

Information obtained for evaluating proposed land developments in accord with the system suggested in this report often can be quite extensive. To make this information as intelligible as possible for the responsible public officials—and other users—requires special care in the form of its presentation. Some initial thoughts on displaying impact data are described here.

As earlier chapters have emphasized, the measures do not provide a means for automatic decisions but rather provide the basis for informed judgments by giving officials and their staffs the pertinent facts of the cases. These facts must then be evaluated in light of the decision makers' understanding of local conditions, problems and objectives.

## IMPACT MEASUREMENT DATA

The presentation of the facts succeeds to the extent that it makes it possible for the viewer to visualize and keep in mind a wide variety of findings. One format for displaying the data in a meaningful way that can be readily grasped is shown in Exhibit 4.

Data are displayed for each relevant impact measure and for each appropriate clientele group. Where possible, ranges should be given for each measure that has considerable uncertainty; this will prevent too much weight or importance from being attached to data that may be dubious and will help indicate the possibly large variety of reasonably likely outcomes. The data also should show whether each estimated impact appears to be consistent with targets included in the community's comprehensive plans. When available and appropriate, standards set by various government agencies or professional groups should be included as frames of reference for judgment, and values that exceed acceptable limits should be flagged.

Additional columns should be added to the exhibit to indicate the cumulative impacts of a set of developments proposed for the same time frame. While the air pollution impacts of a single proposal might be fully acceptable, the overall effect of the series of proposals might appear so critical that modifications would be needed in each individual plan.

In addition to the main exhibit summarizing impacts, charts with further details should be provided as back-ups. These might include before-and-after air quality contours, travel time contours, employment levels by skill category, and the details of cost-revenue analyses, depending on the case.

## PUBLIC FACILITY CAPACITY DATA

A back-up exhibit of particular importance in many instances is one that will show the degree to which a development impinges on the capacity of local government facilities and of private utilities. The relation between impact measures and capacity measures is described on pages 16-17.

*EXHIBIT 5*

## CAPACITY OF PUBLIC FACILITIES

| Type of Public Facility[1] | Percent of Existing Capacity Used | | If Overload, Earliest Time of Relief (in months) |
|---|---|---|---|
| | Before Development | After Development | |
| 1. Main sewage and storm drainage network in the neighborhood | | | |
| 2. Sewage treatment plants | | | |
| 3. Water pumping station | | | |
| 4. Schools | | | |
| 5. Police and fire stations | | | |
| 6. Solid waste disposal facilities | | | |
| 7. Recreation facilities (pools, parks, etc.) | | | |
| 8. Hospitals and other health facilities | | | |
| 9. Major roads | | | |
| 10. Libraries | | | |
| 11. Gas and electric plants or distribution networks | | | |
| 12. Other (specify) | | | |

1. Data should be reported separately for each facility within a type where changes to individual facilities from development can be identified. Under schools, for instance, three elementary schools, two junior highs, and one senior high might be affected. Where a development will be developed in phases, the capacities should be reported by phase.

Exhibit 5 illustrates a format for presenting the capacity data. The types of facilities listed down the first column include those which knowledgeable people believe might be affected by a proposed new development. The next column shows the percent of existing capacity being used. If it is already being used close to—or beyond—capacity, this is a warning that local government must (a) immediately begin adding to capacity, (b) disapprove the development, or (c) warn citizens that the new development will entail a decrease in the quality of public service. If the percent of capacity *after* development appears critical, then the same kinds of choices must be considered. The final column, showing the earliest possible time at which new capacity could be available to relieve any overload problem, puts all of these decisions into a meaningful time frame.

A more comprehensive version of this exhibit would include the availability of adequate personnel to staff facilities, in addition to the provision of physical plant. There may be ample classroom space for additional school children, for instance, yet the quality of service may suffer seriously if the school system has not allowed sufficient lead time for recruiting and paying for additional teachers. Similarly, additional police and fire personnel require training and cannot be produced overnight to fill needs.

The graphic presentation of capacity measures will not only assist officials in deciding land use cases. It will also dramatize the importance of capital improvement programming and budgeting as an integral part of the community land development process.

# PART 2: IMPACT MEASURES-ANALYSIS AND DATA COLLECTION APPROACHES

# CONTENTS PART 2

*Page*

Page

# INTRODUCTION

For each measure listed in Exhibit 1 of the Summary, this section discusses the rationale, problems, and some alternative forms of the measure, where appropriate. Data collection procedures for evaluating past and proposed development are also outlined, but it is beyond the scope of this preliminary work to develop detailed procedures.

A major concern is to provide data collection procedures that are practical and that entail manpower and expenditure levels that local governments can afford. Whenever possible, procedures are suggested that utilize data and skills currently available to most local governments. Overemphasis on data precision can lead to unnecessary data collection costs. The precision and costs should be commensurate with the importance of the decision at hand. Costs for many procedures remain to be determined, however.

For some measures, relatively cheap but crude data collection procedures are identified as well as more detailed, costly procedures. The simpler procedures generally apply to impact analyses of smaller, individual developments. The refined procedures in general would be used only for evaluating large, important, or complex developments, or groups of developments, where higher analysis expenditures are justifiable. Hopefully, lessons learned from the detailed analyses can be used to improve relatively inexpensive methods that are more suitable for the bulk of development decisions.

Data collection procedures for evaluating past and proposed developments are discussed separately where there is a significant difference in methodology.

*In general, the preferred procedure for the retrospective evaluation consists of gathering data both before and after development. If data are not collected prior to development, the previous conditions need to be estimated. The methods for doing this are often similar to those for making estimates forward in time and are not discussed separately.*[1]

Most of the discussion is worded in terms of the evaluation of a single development, but the procedures are generally applicable to evaluating groups of developments as well. The numbering of the chapters and measures in Part 2 correspond to Exhibit 1, pages 10 and 11.

---

1. The italic type used in this paragraph is used throughout Part 2 to enable readers quickly to distinguish material that deals specifically with retrospective evaluations of existing developments (in contrast to the bulk of the discussion which is addressed to the likely impacts of proposed developments).

# I. ECONOMY

Development can affect the local economy in critical ways. Three of the most important are changes in (a) net government fiscal flow (revenues less expenditures), (b) employment, and (c) wealth.[1] The three are closely interrelated. For example, changes in land values may change property tax revenues and thereby the fiscal flow. If a new development stimulates labor force migration from other regions, the fiscal impact differs from a situation where new employment needs are satisfied wholly from the local labor pool. Measures for indicating these three impacts of development are discussed separately.

## PUBLIC FISCAL BALANCE

### Measure 1. Net change in government fiscal flow.

A new development's fiscal impact on local government—the net change in public revenues less operating expenditures and (annualized) capital expenditures—depends to a considerable extent on whether the government will maintain or change its level and quality of services to the new development and to the rest of the community after the development is completed. Concurrently, the level of service to be provided is likely to depend to some extent on the estimated fiscal impacts. That is, the community chooses a level of service based in part on its perception of what it can afford. To further complicate matters, maintaining the same expenditures per capita is not necessarily synonymous with maintaining the same quality of service, since the demands for services and the costs of supplying them may change faster or slower than the rate of residental or business population growth.

The methodology discussed here for assessing fiscal impacts is based on the assumption that current service quality, tax structure, and tax rates are to be maintained. The discussion focuses on evaluating proposed residential development.

*Retrospective analysis would use similar techniques but would have much better estimates for the socio-economic and demographic characteristics of the population of the development, the public services allocated to the development, and so forth.*

Some of the major direct fiscal impacts of commercial and industrial development are discussed, but not the secondary fiscal effects, such as those resulting from the inmigration, commuting, and shopping they stimulate.

A detailed case study illustrating the procedures for estimating fiscal impact has been developed by Muller and Dawson elsewhere.[2]

### Revenue Estimates

Local revenues can be grouped into four categories: (1) revenues associated with real property wealth—the

1. Changes in wealth should preferably include both property values and personal income. Estimating the impact of development on either is difficult, but it seems especially difficult to estimate changes in family income for families in the existing community (outside the development), other than those who will benefit directly from new jobs in the development. We therefore discuss property value changes only, and consider the measures of employment changes as at least a partial proxy for changes in family income.

2. *The Fiscal Impact of Residential and Commercial Development: A Case Study*, The Urban Institute, December 1972. A more detailed description of the state of the art of fiscal impact analysis may be found in Thomas Muller, *Fiscal Impacts of Land Development: Methods and Issues*, The Urban Institute, to be published in 1975.

largest source in most jurisdictions; (2) revenues associated with income and level of consumption, which are comprised primarily of local income, sales, and utility taxes; (3) per capita, per pupil, or other per "population unit" revenues, which are derived from either a per capita tax, or redistribution from higher levels of government; and (4) miscellaneous revenues, which include fees, user charges, fines, licenses, and minor items.

It is useful to identify separately the revenues from business enterprises and revenues from households; and the latter should be further classified as occupants of single family, townhouse, and apartment units.

**Revenues Related to Real Property**

Real property is usually taxed by local governments. In general, the same tax rate applies to both residential and nonresidential property.[3]

Property tax revenues are computed by multiplying the tax rate by the assessed value of property. In most communities, the assessed property value is a percentage of market or full property value. For example, in California, assessments are based on 25 percent of market value. Thus, a $50,000 housing unit should be assessed at $12,500. In most cases, however, there is a difference between the "official" and actual current market value, due to a time lag in updating assessments in an inflationary economy and to other factors. The true "effective tax rate," which should be the basis for estimating additional revenue from new real property, can be computed by dividing the current market value of similar property in the community (estimated from recent real estate sales) by tax payments from the property. The effective tax rate, with few exceptions, is below the official rate. The average effective assessment ratio in California during 1971, as shown in the *1972 Census of Government*, was 20 percent of market value, not the 25 percent ratio required by state legislation. Thus an official or nominal tax rate of $15 per $100 of assessed value, for instance, would amount to a 3 percent effective tax rate, not 3.75 percent as one might assume from use of the official assessment ratio.

The estimated market value of land and structures is usually provided by the developer. It can be compared to values of similar property to determine if it reasonably reflects the local market. The property tax revenues may then be estimated by multiplying the estimated market value of the new real property by the effective tax rate, deducting for exemptions such as homestead, old age-low income, or veteran status. Real property taxes from the current (before development) land use on the development site should be computed and subtracted from the estimated revenue accruing from the proposed development to yield the net change in real property taxes. This is too often neglected in fiscal analysis. Likewise, if the people or businesses displaced by the development leave the jurisdiction, estimates of other tax revenues lost—and expenditures reduced—may be needed.

For income-producing property, such as a large apartment building, property taxes might not be based on the value of the building, but rather on gross or net income. This assessment approach tends to result in higher revenues compared to taxes on the value of the building, unless many units are not occupied.

Changes in property tax revenue may also result if new development induces changes in land values elsewhere in the community. Estimating future land values is discussed in connection with Measure 4. Although such estimates are very difficult to quantify with much confidence, to the extent they can be approximated the associated revenues should be accounted for.

**Revenues Related to Income**

Revenues generated by new development may be directly related to income of residents as with local income taxes. Or they may be indirectly related via consumption as with personal property taxes and local sales taxes. A number of communities impose utility taxes related to income insofar as higher income households have larger housing units and more appliances, and thus consume more energy and water. Excise taxes on specific goods also relate to consumption patterns.

To estimate these income-related taxes, it is necessary to estimate the expected household income of new residents, which may be derived from the relationships between property value and income. These relationships, in turn, can be determined from census data and consumer surveys.[4]

If monthly rent payments for proposed apartment units have been set, income estimates can be derived by assuming rent payments to be a specified share of income.[5] The share of income allocated for housing varies somewhat by location, age, and size of the household, and by type of housing. Annual rental payments also may be estimated as representing, on the average, between one-seventh to one-ninth of the value of the housing unit.

---

3. There are exceptions, as in Minnesota, where industrial and commercial property are taxed at a higher rate than residential property.

4. For a discussion of the demand for housing as a function of income, see F. deLeeuw, "The Demand for Housing: A Review of Cross Section Evidence," *The Review of Economics and Statistics*, Vol. 53, February 1971, pp. 1-10. He found that the value of the new owner-occupied housing was generally between 1.7 and 2.4 times annual income.

5. A number of government publications discuss these proportions. For example, see U.S. Department of Labor, *Three Standards of Living for Urban Families*, Bulletin No. 1570-5, Washington, D.C., 1969.

A more direct method for estimating income of new residents is to examine applications to mortgage institutions, developers, and apartment managers. However, access to these data is extremely difficult because of confidentiality.

*Sales and excise tax* receipts can be estimated–given data on income–from various surveys on expenditures by income class, household size, region, and metropolitan area.[6]

*Income taxes* can be estimated directly by application of appropriate rates to taxable income and size of household. In a few states, local governments can impose a tax on income of residents, or a tax on payrolls, based on place of employment. Many cities in Pennsylvania and Ohio tax income earned in the community. In Maryland, all counties levy an income tax on residents of their jurisdiction. In some states, these local income or payroll taxes are not permitted.

*Personal property* subject to taxation varies widely. The most common items subject to this tax are automobiles and, to a lesser extent, major household goods. Their value can be estimated by their relation to income.[7] In the case of automobiles, it is necessary to ascertain the base used for estimating value (wholesale price, loan value, or market price) and the effective tax rate. Businesses sometimes must pay personal property taxes based on machinery and inventory; these can be roughly estimated if the type of proposed industry is known.

*Utility taxes* are frequently levied as a percentage of utility bills. Estimates of average bills can be based on utility company data for various types of residences, such as large single-family dwellings, smaller single-family dwellings, and apartments.

### Per Capita Revenues

Local governments in some states administer a per capita or "head" tax on all adults. More frequently, local government is the recipient of state or county revenues distributed on the basis of the number of residents or the number of students. For example, profits from the alcoholic beverage sales by the state are distributed to local jurisdictions in Virginia based on population, while sales tax receipts are distributed on the basis of school-age residents. Federal revenue sharing for local jurisdictions, as presently legislated, also uses population as one criterion. (The other criteria are per capita income and tax effort: as income in a community rises relative to other jurisdictions, revenue sharing funds are reduced; an increase in relative tax effort leads to an increase in the federal funds.) Estimates of all per capita taxes should be based on the expected change in local population or school enrollment, applying whatever formulas are used for computing such taxes.

### User Charges, Service Fees, Miscellaneous Revenues

User charges for utility services, other revenues from public utility operations, and fees for public safety, recreational, and other services also can provide substantial revenue to local governments.[8] Such user charges, fees, and fines initially should be allocated between business firms and households. The revenues accruing from households can be approximated on the basis of recent per capita receipts from these sources by the jurisdiction.

## Operating Expenditure Estimates

The importance and scope of local public services for which expenditures must be estimated can differ sharply among and within states. For example, water and sewage utilities and roads and highways are maintained by many localities but not others. Health and welfare often are not city responsibilities, and tend to be small portions of some county budgets. However, they are major expenditure items in cities such as New York or Detroit and in many counties.

The allocation techniques discussed here assume that current local government personnel (teachers, maintenance crews) generally are fully occupied. Thus, a new development that creates additional demand for their services would, in the absence of additional resources, reduce the quality of services. The allocation techniques estimate the cost of maintaining the existing scope and quality of services. The attempt to determine average costs or additional costs for each service, if they can be determined, will be very useful for determining the impacts of new development. It is recognized, however, that existing personnel may be underutilized because of inefficiencies, anticipation of future demand, or other reasons, in which cases judgmental adjustments in operating expenditure estimates would have to be made.

Local operating expenditures can be grouped into those incurred in supplying services used (1) primarily by households, such as education, libraries, health and welfare, and recreation, and those used (2) by both business enterprises and households, such as fire and police, utilities, general government, and transportation.

6. U.S. Department of Labor, Bureau of Labor Statistics, *Survey of Consumer Expenditures*, Report No. 237-88. Washington, D.C., 1965.

7. For data on the relationship between automobile value and personal income, see the most current issue, Bureau of the Census, *Consumer Buying Indicators*, Series P-65, Washington, D.C.

8. For an example of the important role such revenues may play, see T. Muller and G. Dawson, *The Impact of Annexation on City Finances: A Case Study in Richmond, Virginia*, Washington, D.C., The Urban Institute, 1973.

### Household-Related Expenditures–Education

In most local jurisdictions, public education is the largest outlay, as high as 80 percent of operating expenditures in suburban areas of states in which the state governments do not absorb the major share of these burdens. Therefore, the factor which usually determines whether a residential development will result in a fiscal surplus or liability is the projected incremental expenditure for public education.

The two most important factors which determine school enrollment and therefore education expenditures are the type of housing and number of bedrooms per housing unit. A number of studies show how to estimate enrollment on the basis of these two factors.[9] With few exceptions, detached single-family housing units, particularly those with four or more bedrooms, and garden apartments with three bedrooms, have the most school-age children per unit. New detached housing units typically have more children than do older units. The fewest children per unit are found in highrise luxury apartments and condominiums, one-bedroom garden apartments, and two-bedroom townhouses.

In addition to housing type, racial and ethnic characteristics, which are related to children per family and reliance on parochial schools, also influence public school enrollment. Income, which is related to housing type, affects both the demand for higher quality educational services and the reliance on private schools and thus affects public school population and budget.

The distribution of students among grade levels is frequently also a function of housing type. Apartment residents tend to have proportionately more children in elementary grades, and per pupil costs are up to one-third lower in these grades. The use of average per student expenditure throughout the school district, without reference to these differences in grade level distribution for each housing type, is likely to be misleading.

Statistics on children per unit considering the various factors just cited can be developed from school attendance records for the community or similar communities, if they are not already available from the school board. The estimated number of new students per grade times the average cost per student in each grade yields the total estimated educational expenditure.

In communities which support junior colleges and other post-high school education, the impact of new developments on these facilities also needs to be estimated. Enrollment in such institutions is a function of household demographic characteristics and income.

In most states the level of state aid for public education is based, at least in part, on per pupil property values. Thus, a proposed commercial, industrial, or expensive residential development will increase the per pupil property base, decreasing the per pupil state contribution in the future.

### Household-Related Expenditures–Noneducational Services

One simplistic approach to estimating additional noneducational expenditures associated with new households is to assume that the cost per new resident will equal the average cost of these services per existing resident. This easy computation is based on the premise that (1) demand is independent of socioeconomic and demographic characteristics, or that (2) population characteristics of new residents are similar to the base population. It also implies that the unit cost of delivering the services remains constant while demand increases. Numerous studies suggest that these premises are questionable.[10] Characteristics of inmigrants generally differ from those of the base population.[11] The type and unit value of housing can be used to estimate resident characteristics, especially income distribution.

Some of the complexities to be taken into account for improved estimates of noneducational expenditures are discussed in the sections that follow. Cost situations vary too widely from community to community to permit a detailed approach here, but the various references cited will suggest guidelines for interested officials.

*Health and welfare.* Most health and welfare services are directly linked to income. These expenditures tend to be concentrated in older, lower-income areas of a jurisdiction. Since the income of residents in new nonsubsidized housing can be expected to be considerably above the level that would qualify for welfare and health services for the indigent, the demand and thus the incremental cost of social services is likely to be low.

To assess the impact of new residents on social services, the proportion of new households whose income or age is at a level which qualified for social services should be estimated. In addition, the cost of health services available to all residents, regardless of income, should be computed. As population increases, it also may be assumed that the unit cost of social services will rise somewhat, because the cost of living and wages generally are higher in larger communities than in smaller ones.

---

9. See, for example, *Fiscal and Land Use Analysis of Prince George's County*, Doxiadis Urban Systems, Washington, D.C., 1970, and George Sternlieb, *Housing Development and Municipal Costs*, New Brunswick, N.J., Rutgers University Press, 1973.

10. The relationship between population size, density and the unit cost of public services is discussed in Thomas Muller, *Fiscal Issues in Metropolitan Growth*, Washington Metropolitan Council of Governments, Washington, D.C., 1973.

11. Characteristics of inmigrants to large urban areas can be estimated from Bureau of Census *Mobility of Metropolitan Areas*, PC(2)-2c, Washington, D.C., 1973.

*Recreation and libraries.* The demand for certain recreation and library facilities may increase with the inmigration of higher income residents. Concurrently, new developments may provide their own private facilities, reducing the pressure on public services. Some communities plan for a fixed quantity of recreation facilities and open space per capita regardless of private facilities.

Preferably, the additional demand for recreational facilities as a function of age, income, and location of residents would be used to estimate new recreation operating expenditures, modified by special circumstances and characteristics of local policy. In the absence of such data, or, if the policy is equal allocation per capita, the current average cost per household should be allocated to the new development.

**Services Utilized Jointly by Households and Businesses**

Most local services are utilized by both households and business enterprises. As in the case of the household-related services, it is preferable to base cost estimates on actual service additions that can be attributed to the new development. Where circumstances do not allow this, estimates may be based on past expenditures per household, per business employee, or per $1,000 property value.

As a first step for estimating these unit costs, it is useful to identify past expenditures for each sector–households and businesses.[12] In some communities, business enterprises are concentrated in areas with few residential structures, and the services devoted to them may be readily identified. For example, a fire company may serve primarily a central business district, so that all or a large share of that cost can be allocated to business.

In expanding areas, new commercial and perhaps industrial property may be in fairly close proximity to housing, making it difficult to identify the actual resources supplied for each. Several allocation schemes have been devised. The most commonly utilized method is to allocate expenditures for jointly used services–particularly public safety–to business and residences in proportion to their relative property value. An alternative is to rely on the number of employees in business enterprises, as a proportion of total employees and residents, for the allocation to business.[13] Both of these approaches, however, tend to reflect benefit received rather than cost incurred. Where demand data are available, these may be used as the basis of allocation. For example, the number of fire calls associated with business versus the total calls could be used for allocating police and fire services. The proportion of trips generated by residences versus businesses could be used for allocating local transportation services.

Some services are aimed directly at the business sector, such as the testing and sealing of scales. Their costs should be fully allocated to business, even though some benefits may accrue to the residents.

Once historical costs are allocated between business and residences, unit costs can be computed and used for estimating expenditures for new development. Some further comments on estimating costs of the major jointly used services follow.

*General government.* It is difficult to allocate most general government services to a specific development. For small developments, general expenditures can be estimated on a per capita basis.

However, as the community grows, per capita expenditures for general services tend to increase. A wider scope of services is offered, and more highly trained and paid professionals are hired. For large-scale developments, using past per capita costs may thus underestimate the incremental expenditure. The actual allocation should reflect the experience of similar communities in the state which have been growing rapidly in comparison to those where growth has been small. This method of estimating the future cost of services has been applied to a number of communities.[14]

*Fire services.* The need for additional fire service expenditures is determined by the accessibility of new developments to existing fire stations, the current demand level at those stations, and the types of proposed structures.

The frequency of fires per housing unit in new residential developments, based on empirical data, is usually below community averages. However, low density development can require more fire stations per housing unit to offset the longer travel times when housing is spread out. And despite locational differences, certain communities maintain a fixed relationship between firemen and population.[15]

The suggested approach is to allocate incremental operating outlays for fire services on the basis of additional manpower required. If no added personnel are needed, one can estimate the anticipated number of additional fire calls as a proportion of the total number of calls for the fire station nearest the development. This would indicate the

12. A frequent mistake in cost-revenue analysis is to compute per capita (resident) costs by dividing total costs (for businesses and residents) by the number of residents, rather than dividing just the resident-related part of the costs by the number of residents.

13. See, W. Isard and R. Coughlin, *Municipal Costs and Revenue Resulting from Community Growth*, Federal Reserve Bank of Boston, Boston, 1957.

14. See, for example, George Sternlieb, *Housing Development and Municipal Costs*, op. cit.

15. In communities within Santa Clara County, for example, a ratio of one fireman per 1000 residents is maintained. See *Municipal Cost Revenue Analysis*, South Santa Clara Planning Department, 1973.

share of the fire station operating cost to be allocated to the new development.

*Police services.* Per capita police outlays, once some minimum population base is reached, increase as the size of a city increases. It is not known to what extent this is attributable to changes in the level and types of police service provided, socioeconomic characteristics, population density, or other factors. The major factor appears to be the higher level of crime per capita.

New developments characterized in the main by low density housing are likely to have low crime rates.[16] Insofar as crime rates reflect direct demand for police services, the use of a crime index as a proxy for demand is likely to show that the incremental cost in new developments is below the average cost of providing service. Thus using average costs might seem biased. However, police protection extends to roads, shopping areas, and other facilities where residents shop and work. In addition, only a small share of total police calls are directly linked to crimes. Thus average costs may not be as poor a proxy as one might think at first.

Another approach is to base costs on the estimated additional manpower allocated to the new area, adding a proportional share of central administrative and related overhead expenditures. Some communities apply a standard, such as 1.6 uniformed police per 1,000 residents. This implicitly assumes that demand for police services is independent of new population characteristics or the housing mix. It also deals with the development alone, not reflecting its contribution to the higher per capita costs associated with larger communities.

The preferred but somewhat more difficult approach is to estimate the additional manpower likely to be added, based on past experience with similar developments, if any, and discussions with police officials, so that the latest policies can be reflected. To the costs of manpower necessary to serve the new development would be added expected increases in general costs due to the community's increased population, based on experience in other like communities.

## Capital Expenditure Estimates

Three major tasks are involved in estimating the costs of public capital improvements associated with new development.

- The allocation of facility costs between the existing community and the new development.
- Choice of the lifetime and interest rates to be used in annualizing costs of new plant.
- The timing of the new investment.

### Cost Allocation

Capital expenditures associated with new development can be grouped into two categories. First, facilities linked directly with the development, such as new schools, sewer lines, fire stations, and other new facilities to be utilized primarily by the new development. Costs of these facilities can be allocated largely or wholly to the new development. Second, facilities constructed or expanded as part of a capital improvement program which will be shared by existing as well as new residents or enterprises in the jurisdiction. Such facilities could include junior colleges, new sewage or water treatment plants, and health care centers. They are generally not triggered by a single development, unless it is very large.

The costs of the second category pose difficult, classic allocation questions involving consideration of scale economies and the optimum size and timing of new plant construction. The approaches are widely argued and a full discussion cannot be included here. Only a few suggestions must suffice.

If a new facility is part of a capital improvement plan and is initially underutilized in expectation of future growth, only the share of the total cost needed to meet the demands created by the new development should be allocated to it. For example, for a school the number of pupil-years of education required by the development as a percent of the total pupil-years provided by the school over its expected life could be used to allocate the annualized capital costs of the school to the development. This gives some of the benefit from the expected economy of scale to the new development. The balance of the annualized cost, until the facility is fully utilized, is shared by the total community. However, if earlier construction of the new facility is required because of the specific development, the analysis should take account of local funds requiring earlier outlay and the likely costs of construction at different times, including anticipated interest costs on bonds that would be borrowed by the local government for the project.[17]

If the new development uses available space in existing facilities, some would allocate only the short-term incremental cost, some the long-term incremental cost, and some the average cost. Which to use depends on the viewpoint and purpose of the analysis. The short-term

16. See, for example, "Cost Revenue Analysis of New Housing Development in the City of San Diego," *Growth Cost Revenue Studies*, Associated Home Builders, Berkeley, 1973; *Fiscal and Land Use Analysis of Prince George's County*, Doxiadis Urban Systems, Inc., Washington, D.C., 1970.

17. In an inflationary economy, it is frequently advantageous to initiate construction in anticipation of future demands, since annual debt payments are fixed while the tax base is expanding.

incremental cost (which may be zero) reflects the out-of-pocket additional expense for the facility. The long-term incremental cost reflects the costs attributed to new development over the long run, including economies or diseconomies of scale they lead to. The average cost concept assumes each user bears an equal burden.

For either case—whether the new development uses old or new facilities—two separate capital expenditure computations might be made, one emphasizing causation of costs, the other what the community will have to spend. The first would indicate the relative burden on services from the new development, the second the changes in fiscal outlays that would be needed.

In some cases, a new development triggers a new capital investment that will be used by all of the community, and that will raise the per capita cost to the community for a service. An example is a tertiary sewage treatment plant required to keep water pollution below some limit. In most communities the practice is to distribute the cost of such facilities equally among all users. The cost for fiscal impact analysis purposes might be allocated to the entire community, but in some cases the costs might be allocated to the new development—it depends on the reasons for adding the plant and whether overall service quality improves or remains the same.

Facilities fully utilized prior to new development, such as public schools, should not be considered as part of the capital cost attributable to the new development.

**Annualizing Costs**

There are three methods of paying for major capital projects: (1) general revenues from current tax receipts, (2) general obligation or revenue bonds, and (3) current revenue combined with general obligation or revenue bonds.[18]

Whether capital expenditures, which provide current as well as future benefits, should be paid from current revenues or over an extended time period, involves issues of equity, since the composition of the population using the capital improvements undergoes change during the useful life of the investment.[19] Most large communities—for both fiscal and political reasons—tend to borrow funds, particularly for school facilities.

The method of financing chosen by a jurisdiction influences the short-term and long-term costs of capital investment. In a slow-growing jurisdiction, a substantial portion of capital needs can be met from current revenues, on a "pay as you go" basis. Capital expenditures for such services as publicly owned utilities are usually self-financing from user charges through revenue bonds, and thus impose no direct burden on the public sector fiscal structure. However, major capital costs, for services not funded by user charges, particularly in areas of rapid growth, cannot be financed from current funds. Therefore, general obligation bonds are issued for a selected payback period.

The bond repayment periods selected by communities generally vary between 20 and 30 years. A suggested approach for determining per annum cost involves calculating the straight line amortization of capital over the useful life of the investment and adding the interest on the average balance outstanding. The interest rate selected when computing annualized capital expenditures should reflect the bond market at the time of the analysis. In 1973, interest rates for communities with a high bond rating fluctuated between 4.7 and 5.5 percent. (These percentages are considerably below the private market rate, since the interest on these bonds is not subjected to federal income taxes.)

An alternative approach for computing the capital cost would be to estimate the useful economic life of the investment (excluding the value of the land), independent of the bond repayment period. Presumably, if the actual economic life could be estimated, the annual interest charges on a bond could be added to the amortized per annum economic life of the project. Thus, if bonds for a project had a 30-year repayment period, but the useful economic life of the project was 40 years, the annual capital costs could be reduced, although the difference would not be substantial. Technological and other changes may result in a shorter useful economic life for a capital investment than initially projected. In addition, elements of a particular project are likely to have differing economic life spans. As a result, basing estimates on the anticipated economic life of a project has practical limitations. Whatever method of annualization is used should be clearly stated, since it is often the basis for criticism in comparing fiscal flows.

**Timing of Investment**

Unless existing facilities are underutilized, increases in population or business enterprise expansion require immediate new public and private sector capital investment. The alternative would be a reduction in the level and quality of existing services, such as double school sessions, increased traffic congestion, or overcrowded recreational facilities.

In areas of rapid growth, public infrastructure investments frequently lag behind population increases because of public sector fiscal limitations, such as legal limits on borrowing; lag in revenues from new development; the

18. Revenue bonds are those bonds secured with income received by a jurisdiction from the earnings of a revenue-producing enterprise, such as waterworks. General obligation bonds are secured by an unconditional pledge of a jurisdiction's credit, including its taxing power.

19. For a theoretical discussion of public debt issues, see R. A. Musgrave, *The Theory of Public Finance,* New York, McGraw Hill, 1959.

initial diseconomies of scale (i.e., underutilization) associated with new facilities; or because of inadequate planning. As a result, there is often a short-term degradation in the provision of public services. If this is expected to be the case, it should be reflected in the various measures (17-36) of service quality.

## EMPLOYMENT

### Measure 2. Number of new long-term and short-term jobs provided.

### Measure 3. Change in the numbers and percent employed, unemployed, and underemployed.

The traditional measure of the impact of a new development on employment is the estimated total number of jobs created. This measure is of interest and relatively easy to estimate, but it does not directly reflect the impact of the development on employment opportunities for the present citizens of the community. It does not indicate whether the new jobs will be taken by persons from outside the community or by persons within the community. In the latter case, will old jobs be wiped out or will new openings be created and left for others to fill?

To deal with these matters requires explicit estimates of the impact of the development on unemployment and underemployment as well as on the new long-term and short-term jobs added to the community. Even if the impact on unemployment and underemployment can be only crudely estimated, as is likely, it will help provide a more balanced impression of the significance of the new jobs. Note that a net addition of jobs to a community reduces the *percentage* unemployed, even if no one currently unemployed gets a job. For this reason, absolute as well as percentage changes should be identified.

Industrial and commercial development often directly create additional jobs. Residential development only creates jobs indirectly, except for those utilized in the construction itself.[20] It is useful, therefore, to treat the employment effects of these types of development separately.

20. It is generally assumed that the demand for residential construction (except retirement communities, tourist facilities, or vacation homes) follows employment opportunities. It is possible but rare that a shortage of housing precludes further industrial/ commercial development. In some cases, the availability of a wide range of housing may attract industry, but this is not the typical situation. Therefore, residential development generally does not result in creating long-term employment in the private sector directly. However, it may indirectly create public sector jobs for police, firefighters, teachers, etc., and private sector jobs servicing household needs to the extent that the development attracts new residents to the community.

### Industrial and Commercial Development

Nonresidential development may bring three types of employment to the community: (1) short-term jobs, related to construction of the development and its associated public and private infrastructure such as utility lines, roads, power plant extensions, and telephone switching,[21] (2) long-term direct employment provided by new or expanded business enterprises, and (3) secondary impacts due to increased economic activity stimulated by the development.

#### Short-Term

Construction-related short-term employment may offer little help to those in the community who are presently underemployed or unemployed, though it may prevent their number from increasing. The unemployed often do not have the necessary skill levels to participate. The number of additional short-term jobs provided to the community depends on the local labor market and trade union practices.

*Short-term employment opportunities provided by past development can be estimated from data provided by organizations which participated in construction and related activities. The employment actually generated may differ from original estimates as a result of construction delays, modifications of plans, changes in union contracts, and changes in the skill mix of workers used, not to mention unrealistic initial estimates. Local communities should find it useful to occasionally determine the accuracy of such estimates in retrospect.*

The likely number of short-term, construction-related jobs resulting from proposed development may be estimated from similar projects previously completed. A second approach is to estimate the labor share of the total expected construction costs, and then to convert this into man-years based on average construction labor costs. Data on the labor portions of total costs for various types of construction are compiled by trade associations and government agencies. A third approach is to estimate the number of man-hours for plumbers, electricians, and other trades per building unit based on past trends. The developer—who probably already will have done the computation—may be a source for these data.

#### Long-Term

Employment impacts of industrial and commercial developments in the long run depend on the number of new jobs generated, the availability in the community of the

21. Though called short-term, these jobs are of course often long-term for the employee involved because of continual development. But if development stopped, it is likely that these jobs would, too.

*[Paragraphs in italics deal with retrospective analyses]*

skills needed, and the proportion of these jobs likely to be filled by community residents, commuters, or inmigrants. It further depends on whether local persons who fill the new jobs would otherwise be unemployed, would just be entering or reentering the labor force (as in the case of teenagers and wives of heads of household who were not previously working or seeking work), or changing employment within the community. In the latter case, the impact further depends on whether the jobs left behind are filled, and if so, whether from within the community. Unfortunately, data on the unemployed and underemployed, particularly within local jurisdictions, are usually poor.

Data on the new long-term employment expected in the new development may be available directly from its planned businesses. Most firms estimate the number of employees needed for their expected level of output or service. It may be useful for the local government to request that proposed enterprises provide information on the approximate number, type, and gross wage structure of employees they anticipate, identifying the number and types of workers to be imported (including transfers within the organization) and the number and types to be hired locally or within commuting distance. Otherwise, the proportion of new jobs likely to go to people within the community as opposed to those outside but within commuting distance may be estimated based on past experience with similar industries. The proportion of jobs going to persons outside commuting distance versus those within range is much trickier to estimate, since it is dependent on the relative slack in the labor markets in communities that are within and outside commuting distance.

Details on the number of expected jobs will not be available when the specific enterprises that will occupy the development are unknown, or when they are unwilling to provide this somewhat sensitive information. As an alternative, the number and skill mix of new jobs may be roughly estimated from the assumed or likely types of businesses, based on estimates of the floor space, or (though less frequently available) expected payroll or sales volume. Estimates of floor space per employee are available by type of industry.[22] Estimates of the wage structure of new businesses can be based on average wage rates published by industry type.[23] The census also provides payroll data for blue collar and white collar labor for metropolitan areas, cities, and counties.[24] However, new facilities tend to incorporate the latest technology, and may have higher skilled labor, higher wages and less employees per unit of output than the averages listed by industry in the published sources. In fact, relocation of a business within a jurisdiction may lead to a net loss of employment opportunities because of the substitution of capital for labor, unless relocation is accompanied by expansion of output. On the other hand, if a business is relocating from a high wage area to take advantage of the availability of labor, then a more labor-intensive job production process might be used.

*Evaluating the effect of past industrial and commercial development on long-term unemployment and underemployment may be undertaken with data provided by employers within the project site or by a survey among new employees there to determine their prior work location and work status. For large developments, one might check for detectable changes in overall community unemployment statistics.*

Where possible, various categories of unemployment status should be distinguished. For example, a housewife who did not seek work until a new enterprise located within commuting distance for her is defined by the Department of Labor as moving into employment from outside the labor force, not from the ranks of the unemployed. Unemployed people may be categorized as "frictionally unemployed"—that is, temporarily between jobs, or having difficulty getting their first job—or as structural, "hard core" jobless, a more permanent and more serious problem. Still others are underemployed—holding jobs below their capacity due to immobility, discrimination, tight job markets, or other reasons.

**Secondary Impacts**

Employment, particularly in retain business and services, may result from new development via the so-called multiplier effect. Each new primary job created by industrial and commercial development may stimulate added service jobs. There also may be increased demand for labor in industries supplying materials for construction or for use by the new industry, though these jobs may fall largely outside the immediate community.

The secondary employment impacts within the community can best be estimated from data on previous expansions that show growth of service industries in relation to the increase of primary jobs. Particularly in smaller communities, a larger share of the secondary employment may "leak out" to other areas.

*Secondary employment impacts for specific past developments will usually be too diffuse to identify explicitly. Exceptions would be special circumstances, as when the new development was large and relatively isolated, leading to the creation of small service businesses in its immediate vicinity.*

---

22. For example, see Connecticut Development Group, Inc., *Cost-Revenue Impact Analysis for Residential Developments, New Haven*, 1973.

23. U.S. Bureau of the Census, *County Business Patterns*, published annually, see most recent report.

24. U.S. Bureau of the Census, *Census of Manufacturing*, see most recent five-year Census or most recent annual survey.

## Residential Development

Estimating construction-related short-term employment from residential development is similar to the procedure used for industrial and commercial development.[25]

Secondary impacts on public employment anticipated for some services can be obtained from the government agencies. For example, the board of education might estimate the additional teachers to be hired as the result of a new housing development. For other public services, such as police and fire, the increased personnel should probably be prorated according to population, or on whatever basis would be consistent with the allocation of costs used for the fiscal flow analysis (see the expenditure estimates in Measure 1).

Secondary impacts on private sector employment usually cannot be estimated directly. In some cases, such as when a concentration of housing is likely to lead to the building of a shopping center or other service facilities, new employment can be crudely estimated based on the proportion of total sales to consumers from the new development. Alternatively, more or less standard multipliers for relating secondary to primary employment can be used.[26]

## Stability

In addition to the number of jobs created for the community, it is important for a community to consider the stability of the jobs created. Employment in some types of industry, such as utilities, government, and nondurable goods production, is more stable than in others, such as defense or durable goods production. A community reduces the risk of high unemployment by attracting a wide spectrum of enterprises, including those not sensitive to short-term changes in the economy. The stability of a particular enterprise in a community also depends on factors independent of the economy as a whole—such as the quality of management, the quality of union organization, and the supply of workers with necessary skills.

*Stability of jobs associated with past developments can be estimated by comparing how many workers were laid off due to cutbacks and the rate of expansion of the local labor force during the two or three years after those developments were completed.*

To estimate the stability of the new jobs, data on the experience of industries to be located in the new development should be examined. The U.S. Bureau of Labor Statistics publishes detailed data on rates of employment by industry.

25. For examples of typical labor requirements, see R. Ball, "Labor Requirements for Construction of Single Family Houses," *Monthly Labor Review*, September 1971, pp. 12-17.

26. See, for example, Charles B. Garrison, "New Industry in Small Towns: The Impact of Local Government," *National Tax Journal*, December 1971, pp. 493-505.

# WEALTH

## Measure 4. Change in land values.

Development may have a sharp impact on land values in its vicinity—either up or down, though usually up. The degree of impact is a function of many factors, including the prospects of further development, zoning policies, the demand for land for various purposes, changes in economic activity generated by the development, accessibility, available amenities, and the type of land use change. The impacts on land values usually diminish with distance from the development.

A number of studies have undertaken to quantify the relationship of various factors to land values.[27] While the major reasons for differences in land value from one area to another have been reasonably well established, less is known about the quantitative impact of new developments on surrounding land values, although some studies have examined the relationship.[28]

*One approach for estimating the impact of past development on values of nearby property is to compare sales data for similar properties before and after the development. Prices should be adjusted for inflation. A second approach is to examine property assessment records before and after development to determine how local appraisers anticipated the impact of the new development on surrounding property values relative to assessments for similar properties that have not been affected by development in their immediate vicinity. It should be noted also that public improvements—roads, sewers, parks, etc.—may have a greater impact on property values than the new developments themselves, although the two are closely related.*[29]

27. See, for example, William J. Stull, "An Essay on Externalities, Property Values and Urban Zoning," unpublished Ph.D. dissertation, Massachusetts Institute of Technology, 1971. Findings discussed in *Cost-Revenue Impact Analysis for Residential Developments*, The Connecticut Development Group, Inc., 1973. Also E.F. Brigham, *A Model of Residential Land Values*, RAND Corporation RM-4043-RC, 1964; and D.M. Grether and P. Mieszkowski, "Determinants of Real Estate Values," *Journal of Urban Economics*, Vol. 1, No. 2, May 1974, pp. 127-146.

28. See, for example, Mohammed A. Qadeer, "Local Land Market and a New Town: Columbia's Impact on Land Prices in Howard County, Maryland," *AIP Journal*, March 1974, pp. 110-123.

29. An example of land price increases that resulted from public improvements may be found in *The Socio-Economic Impact of the Capital Beltway on Northern Virginia*, University of Virginia, 1968.

*[Paragraphs in italics deal with retrospective analyses]*

Rough estimates of property value changes to be expected in the vicinity of a proposed development can be made by analogy to past experience with similar developments. Undoubtedly, precise estimates of future property value changes are well beyond the state of the art for most situations in most communities. Nevertheless, an attempt should be made to at least identify areas likely to increase or decrease in value, and the likely degree of change, so as to help identify those clientele groups that are likely to benefit or lose from the development. Property values estimates also are needed for cost-revenue analysis, to estimate changes in property tax revenues.

Factors associated with new development which directly affect land values include the following: type of development, number of new households, and remaining land available for more intensive uses.

### Type of New Development

The addition of detached housing units in an area where single-family housing already predominates may increase property values. This is what tends to happen when a type of development occurs that reinforces people's expectations. If the same low-density residential area witnesses the construction of some highrise apartments or industrial facilities, a mixed impact on property values may result. To homeowners who are concerned about increased congestion, pollution, or other possible problems, the area may suddenly appear less attractive, and their decision to sell out and move may cause the prices of their homes to drop. At the same time, land values in the area may rise because of the anticipation among investors that additional intensive development of apartments or industry is likely to follow.

### Number of Households in the Development

New development with a large number and concentration of households will increase the pressure to use nearby land for commercial uses, such as shopping centers, banks, and gasoline stations, boosting the value of the land.

### Remaining Land Available for Development

The price of land in areas of rapid growth usually increases as the amount of land zoned and available for development, particularly for intensive development, diminishes. For example, if land zoned for high density apartments is limited relative to demand, its value will rise sharply as the artifically restricted supply is used up. However, if ample land is available, and rezoning is easy to obtain, its value will not increase as much as a result of development, since its owners already would be pricing it according to the market for its potentially more intensive use.[30]

Additional factors which can influence land values in areas of growth include the following: availability of public facilities, property taxes, and the physical characteristics of the land.

### Availability of Public Facilities

Underutilized facilities such as schools, roads, fire stations, and utilities (particularly sewage treatment plants) influence nearby land values by making further development more immediately feasible.

### Property Taxes

High property taxes tend to lower land prices and to discourage the long-term holding of sites that are not being used in accord with their full potential. If a new development requires public services that cost more than the new tax revenues it generates and necessitates a general increase in the community's property tax rate, this will reduce the net return on most properties and reduce their selling price. Low property taxes, on the other hand, make it less costly for owners to hold land idle, tending to reduce the effective supply and to raise the cost of land available for development.

### Physical Characteristics of Land

Land with desirable physical characteristics appreciates faster than land with neutral or negative features because it is cheaper or faster to develop or is environmentally more appealing. For example, nearby residential development is likely to cause wooded land to appreciate faster than land without trees. Steeply sloped or very rocky land appreciates more slowly than average—unless the view compensates for the construction disadvantages. Where sewers are not available, the percolation capacity of the soil may influence its rate of increase.

30. For a further discussion of the issue, see M. Neutze, *The Suburban Apartment Boom*, Baltimore, Johns Hopkins University Press, 1968.

# II. NATURAL ENVIRONMENT

The general intent of this report is to focus on how development affects the citizenry rather than on intermediate indicators. Environmental factors, however, are treated directly for two main reasons, even though they are intermediate indicators of some impacts. First, they are important in their own right as the nation is recognizing that the condition of the earth is an essential part of the human heritage to be passed on. Second, while it becomes increasingly evident that changes in the natural environment may strongly affect the health, economics, aesthetics, and leisure opportunities of a community, it is not clear how to translate these specific development impacts on the environment with any degree of certainty.

## AIR POLLUTION

**Measure 5. Change in the level of air pollutants and change in the number of people at risk or bothered by air pollution.**

Residential developments affect air pollution through several types of emissions:

- From internal combustion engines, as a result of changing the number, length, distribution, and mode of trips.
- From fuel burning within the development for heating and cooling.
- From power plants that serve the development.
- From solid waste disposal plants that serve the development.
- From dust and wind erosion of soil caused by construction or by changes in the amount of land cover.

Industrial and commercial developments have these same pollution modes, plus the by-products of industrial processes that are vented to the air. Both types of developments also may increase pollution indirectly by stimulating activity in the community generally.

The net change in levels and distribution of pollution caused by the development will depend on the net number of inmigrants attracted; changes in the relative location of residential, work and shopping sites (and thereby the amount and distribution of traffic); the displacement or elimination of pollution caused by the previous land use; the location relative to local winds and other climatic conditions; and whether the development represents an addition or just a shift of activities within the community.[1]

Three aspects of air pollution associated with developments should be estimated:

- The change in **levels of air pollutants** considered hazardous to health or damaging to property (including carbon monoxide, sulfur oxides, hydrocarbons, particulates, nitrogen oxides, photochemical oxidants).
- The effect on **visual aesthetics,** in terms of opacity and shade of emitted smoke plumes

1. To illustrate the last point, moving a factory to better quarters across the street from where it was might have little impact on air quality in its neighborhood. The result depends on whether it expanded production, changed processes, what it replaced at the new location, and what filled in behind it at the old location.

(the blacker and denser the smoke, the more offensive it is to most people).

- The intensity of **unpleasant odors.**

For the changes in air pollutants, the increased number of people affected should also be estimated, preferably in terms of their frequency and duration of exposure to pollution above specified levels.[2] These levels may be local, state, or national standards representing best estimates of the different levels that may impact health or aesthetics. For example, New York City has defined an air quality index which categorizes pollutant levels as "good, acceptable, unsatisfactory, or unhealthy."[3]

For most small developments the analysis should probably center on changes in the immediate vicinity since the small increment of pollutants is not likely to be detectable elsewhere. Nevertheless, the cumulative effects of development require attention; small increments that could be dismissed as insignificant when viewed individually may, as a whole, substantially change overall air quality.

*The collection of data about the impact of previous development on air quality is often facilitated by the fact that many cities regularly monitor air pollutants at a few sampling points. These measurements may suffice for making gross estimates of the effects of development on air quality. But the sampling stations are unlikely to be in the "right" places for identifying localized effects of specific developments. And there probably will not be enough sampling stations to allow direct construction of pollution contour maps which are useful for estimating the number of persons affected.*[4]

*Mobile monitoring stations can be used to fill some of the gaps. They can be placed at suspected "worst" spots, in the immediate vicinity of the development, at locations likely to reflect the hazard faced by the largest number of people, or at locations most important for extrapolating pollution contours. Care must be taken in choosing the location, height, time of day, weather condition, etc., to help ensure that the measurements will be meaningful.*

*Physically measured changes in air quality are likely to result from a combination of development effects of changes in emission controls, power usage, vehicle usage, and other factors in the rest of the community. It will be necessary, therefore, to allocate the measured changes between the development in question and outside causes, except perhaps for developments that are very large relative to their community, or for pollutants introduced by the development that are new to the community and easily recognized as such.*

*Where an allocation of measured changes in pollution between the development and other factors is necessary, it may be based on estimates of the onsite and offsite pollutants generated by the development relative to the pollutants generated from other sources. These estimates of relative proportions may range from very crude guesses at one extreme to estimates based on measured emissions from point sources, counts of vehicles, and the use of pollutant dispersion models (such as discussed below for estimating effects from proposed developments).*[5]

*Where physical measurements of changes in air quality are not feasible, estimating procedures would again be similar to those for proposed developments. This is likely to be the case even in communities with mobile measuring stations since an adequate number of direct measurements for estimating pollution contours will usually be too expensive and time consuming for a single development.*

*If pollution contour maps are developed either by physical measurements or dispersion models or a combination of both, they may then be overlayed on residential density maps to estimate the number of residents exposed to unsatisfactory levels more than some chosen number of times per year. The average number of people travelling through high pollutant areas on each day of the week should be considered in addition to residents of those areas in determining the number of people affected. At present, it will probably not be possible to produce meaningful contour maps for more than a few pollutants such as carbon monoxide, though much research attention is being devoted to improving methodologies for other pollutants.*

*Much air quality testing is already required by local, state, or federal codes. Data on acceptable pollution ranges from different sources are now available from environmental protection agencies. Methods for physical sampling and analysis of air pollutants are generally well known and are not discussed further here.*[6]

---

2. There are still major questions as to what pollution levels constitute hazards, especially in the long run. Therefore, whenever the number of people at risk is estimated, the criteria used in defining various risks levels should be specified, too.

3. Each of the four New York City air quality levels is defined in terms of an allowable range for each of six pollutants, as described in "Air Pollution Control News," *The American City*, August 1972, p. 22.

4. Pollution contour maps consist of lines of equal pollutant levels. They are analogous to weather maps which show lines of equal air pressure.

5. Note that emissions measured at the source–at the smokestack, for example–are not the same as measurements of air quality taken at various other community locations.

6. For general reference documents, see J. Juda, et al. *Methodology of Atmospheric Air Pollution Measurement I.*, National Science Foundation, Washington, D.C., 1971 and R.A. McCormick, *Air Pollution Measurement*, Environmental Protection Agency, Division of Meteorology, 1972.

*[Paragraphs in italics deal with retrospective analyses]*

*The* **shade and opacity of smoke** *emitted from developments can be quickly determined by a trained inspector making comparisons with a Ringelmann Chart, which is simply a set of illustrations of different densities.*[7]

*The* **intensity of odors** *can most simply be determined by a "trained nose" using a zero-to-four scale, such as follows:*[8]

*0–No sensation of odor.*

*1–Just detectable odor (the threshold dilution).*

*2–Distinct and definite odor whose unpleasant characteristics are revealed or foreshadowed (the recognition threshold).*

*3–Odor strong enough to cause a person to attempt to avoid it completely.*

*4–Odor so strong as to be overpowering and intolerable for any length of time.*

Estimating changes in air quality from proposed developments can be broken into several steps: (1) estimating additional or reduced emissions caused by the development, (2) translating these emissions into estimates of air quality, and (3) computing the changes in the number of people likely to be exposed to air pollution levels considered unsafe or unpleasant.

## Estimating Emissions

The emissions caused by the development can be estimated from the net change in the number of polluting sources, and the pollutants emitted per pound of material consumed per hour. The estimated emission rates must be modified according to the type of pollution control devices likely to be used, for example, in commercial heating plants or factory production processes. Emissions associated with the previous use of the site also should be estimated or measured to assess the net effect of the new development, which in some cases might be a reduction in pollution.

### Vehicular Traffic

Vehicular emissions are a function of the number of vehicle trips per hour, average vehicle speed, and the trip length. Thus, increased traffic congestion–which may reduce average speeds–as well as the increased car trips generated by the development need to be considered.

For determining the change in vehicular emissions in the entire community, and not just in the vicinity of the development, assumptions must be made about the net number of car trips and their distribution within the community. For example, if some deteriorated houses were demolished to make way for open space, and the residents were relocated across town, there might be a shift in distribution of pollution but little change in gross overall average pollution, or in the number of people affected.

Note that the emissions per pound of fuel are changing annually as the proportion of cars without pollution controls are reduced to conform with stiffer emission standards.[9]

### Onsite Residential Heating and Cooling Systems

Emissions from onsite systems can be computed from the pounds of gas or oil consumed per day (by season), times the emissions per pound given off in the use of these fuels.[10]

### Solid Waste Incineration

Emissions from incineration can be estimated based on the pounds of refuse generated per day. This in turn can be estimated from rules of thumb about pounds per person and the expected emissions per pound, or from the type and size of the establishment in the case of business. Data are available on the pounds of contaminants added to the air per ton of refuse burned.[11] Adjustments must be made for control devices and processes used.

### Electrical Power

Increased emissions from this source can be estimated according to the average daily power requirements and the fuel used to generate electricity locally.[12]

---

7. Kudlich, R., *Ringelmann Smoke Chart*, Information Circular 7718., U.S. Department of Interior, Bureau of Mines, revised by C.R. Burdick, 1955.

8. J. De Chiara and L. Koppelman, *Planning Design Criteria*, New York, Van Nostrand Reinhold, 1969, p. 336.

9. Auto emission prediction is discussed in detail in: Jacobsen, Willis E., *Automotive Emissions*, McLean, Va., MTR-6009, Vol. 2, Mitre Corporation, 1971, and Ott, Wayne, John F. Clarke, and Guntis Ozolins, *Calculating Future Carbon Monoxide Emissions and Concentrations from Urban Traffic Data*, U.S. Department of Health, Education, and Welfare, National Air Pollution Control Administration, Durham, North Carolina, 1967.

10. As an example of the types of data available on emissions per pound, see American Public Health Association, Inc., *Guide to the Appraisal and Control of Air Pollution*, New York, 1969, p. 65.

11. Ibid., contains a table of contaminants per ton burned, but note that the numbers vary for various disposal processes and pollution controls.

12. U.S. Environmental Protection Agency, *Guide for Compiling a Comprehensive Emission Inventory*. (PB212-231, APTD-1135), Washington, D.C., 1972, and William Vatavuk, *Control Devices Workbook*, OPA (APTD-15010), 1974.

**Industry**

Industrial emissions can be estimated according to projected production, based on analyses that already exist for the emissions from most industrial processes.[13] If possible, smoke or odors likely to be present should be noted, based on past experience with similar industrial processes.

### Estimating Air Quality Changes

Gross approximations of general air quality effects can be estimated from emission data by assuming a linear relationship between increases in emissions and the resultant changes in ambient air quality levels. Thus, if the ratio of current emissions to current ambient levels is determined, it may be assumed the same ratio will hold for the future. This rough level of analysis is likely to be appropriate for small developments assessed one at a time. Emphasis would tend to be on the area near the development, though local meteorological conditions must be considered for determining the appropriateness of this simple choice.

To predict more accurately the effect of additional air pollution sources on air quality, diffusion models may be needed. These incorporate data on location, type, and amount of emissions; meterological conditions; and in some cases, topographical or surface conditions. For some types of pollutants they must also consider physical and chemical changes as the pollutants interact with the atmosphere and sunlight. The Environmental Protection Agency has developed or modified six diffusion models for emissions from point sources, area sources (i.e., all emissions averaged over an area), and line sources (e.g., highways).[14] There remains a good deal of controversy as to the accuracy of these models. Research to improve and validate them is underway in many organizations.

### Estimating the Number of People Affected

Changes in air quality should be translated into terms of changes in the number of people likely to be exposed to pollution levels considered unsafe or uncomfortable. Pollution contour maps, described in connection with past developments, may be overlaid on population maps to aid in estimating the number of residents living in areas with high pollution levels. Estimates preferably should include the number of people who travel through and work in areas of high pollution.

Data from air diffusion models, cited earlier, can be used to prepare pollution contour maps. When such models are not appropriate, as in the case of smaller developments, an attempt should still be made to estimate how many people will be affected by changes in air quality.

The scientific community, it has been noted, is not in full agreement as to what constitutes danger levels of various pollutants. Air quality danger thresholds, therefore, should be updated as new, improved information becomes available.

## WATER POLLUTION

**Measure 6. Change in the level of water pollutants, change in tolerable types of use, and number of persons affected, for each body of water.**

Developments may add to the pollution of bodies of water in many ways. The amounts and nature of wastes may overwhelm local sewage treatment facilities. Where septic tanks are used, the wastes generated may exceed the capability of the soil to remove or degrade wastes, and affect underground and surface waters. Changes in land contours, vegetation, and permeable land cover during and after construction may increase the amount and content of storm runoff.

Water pollution components to be measured for a body of water include suspended and dissolved solids, dissolved oxygen, toxic materials, and the physicial characteristics such as color, odor, turbidity, and temperature. These have been widely discussed and do not require elaboration here. However, as with air pollution, it is strongly recommended that changes in water pollution be translated into terms that make the impact on the community more readily understandable, and not left in technical physical or chemical terms such as "parts per million." For example, each local body of water might be assessed in the following terms:

13. Ibid. Also, for emissions from various industrial processes, R.L. Duprey, *Compilation of Air Pollutant Emission Factors*, U.S. Department of Health, Education and Welfare, PHC Publication No. 999-AP-42, Durham, North Carolina, 1968.

14. Computer programs for these models are now available for a nominal charge. For information, write Ronald E. Ruff, Meteorology Lab, EPA Environmental Research Center, Research Triangle Park, Raleigh, North Carolina.

The APRAC-IA Urban Diffusion Model Computer Program developed at Stanford Research Institute is one of these models. It estimates carbon monoxide concentrations in an urban area based on two types of input variables: estimated traffic volumes (expressed in vehicles per hour) on a network of road segments in the area and environs; and local meteorological conditions, largely obtainable from a local airport. The program computes average hourly pollutants for 600 points that can be positioned at the user's discretion. This program has been validated for San Jose and St. Louis, with relatively good correlations between predicted and actual levels of pollution. For a description, "An Urban Diffusion Simulation Model for Carbon Monoxide," *Journal of the Air Pollution Control Association*, Vol. 23, No. 6, June 1973, pp. 490-498. R.L. Mancuso and F.L. Ludwig, *User's Manual for the APRAC-1A Urban Diffusion Model Computer Program*, Stanford Research Institute, Menlo Park, California, 1972. Among its main virtues are the low cost of running the model, the use of usually available inputs, and the ability to connect the output to a contour plotting routine that will draw isopleths.

- **Changes in the highest safe uses.** Are there former uses which the body of water can no longer serve? For example, is the river, lake or stream no longer safe for drinking? swimming? eating its fish? water skiing? boating? any of these?[15] Are there uses that have become safe as a result of development, perhaps due to new public or private pollution controls?

- **Change in aesthetically tolerable uses.** Although still safe, a body of water may become unpleasant for various recreational activities after development. On the other hand, development may enhance use. Any changes in acceptable uses would be noted. For example, does the water look or smell bad enough to deter swimmers? boaters? fishermen? sightseers along the bank?[16]

- **Ecological changes.** Changes in pollution and physical characteristics of the water may affect water life directly or through changes in the food chain. Changes in the food chain and in the quantity and quality of fish, shellfish, and water animals would be reported. This might also be included as part of Measures 9 and 10, which describe changes in wildlife.

## Data Collection for Past Development

*Data on changes in water quality are sometimes obtainable from governmental agencies which regularly monitor water pollution by components. Changes in pollution caused by overloading treatment facilities or new treatment processes are directly measurable. The extent to which the additional pollution comes from the development, as opposed to being caused by increased sewage volume communitywide, can be estimated from data on water usage per year per residence and business. These data are usually available from local water and sewer departments. Effluents from industrial development can be and often are monitored directly by local or higher authorities.*

*Changes in water pollution from runoffs during and after construction are difficult to attribute to a particular source except in special circumstances. Short-term, construction-related effects can be estimated qualitatively based on onsite inspections by local government inspectors or others during construction. Long-term effects on water quality are much more difficult to estimate and methods are still in the research stage.*

*Pollution levels, once measured or estimated, can then be translated into the "highest safe use," and "aesthetically tolerable uses" by comparing the estimated pollutant levels against the latest standards for safe and tolerable levels.*[17]

*The number of people affected by changes in water pollution can be estimated from citizen surveys indicating intensities of usage for various bodies of water, or by direct onsite observation.*

## Data Collection for Proposed Development

The basic steps are similar to those for air pollution: estimation of net changes in effluents to each body of water likely to be affected; computation of the dispersion and interaction of the new pollutants with the existing conditions; and estimation of the number of people likely to be affected.

Total gallons of sewage per day for residential and commercial development can be estimated from the size of the residence or expected establishments and known averages of sewage generated per person (or type and size of establishment) per day.[18] Based on current and planned sewage treatment capacities and efficiencies, estimates can be made of whether the added sewage will or will not cause further water pollution.

Given the location and amount of expected effluents, models for the various types of bodies of water can convert these data into estimates of pollution over space and time. Simple and inexpensive general models do exist but are limited to only a few parameters, such as dissolved oxygen.[19] Models which treat complex phenomena such as nutrient cycles are usually calibrated to a specific body of water.

For a given body of water, the number of people likely to be affected can be approximated by the number of predevelopment users for each activity that will be curtailed or made less pleasant by a change in water quality.

---

15. For one detailed set of water safety criteria see, J.E. McKee and H.W. Wolf, Eds., *Water Quality Criteria,* Second Edition, Publication 3-A, The Resources Agency of California, State Water Quality Control Board, 1963. Again the reader is cautioned that standards are continually changing and a subject of much controversy.

16. For a discussion of pollution levels that seem to deter most people from various water-related recreational activities, see D.W. Bishop and R. Aukermann, *Water Quality Criteria for Selected Recreational Uses*, Research Report No. 33, University of Illinois Water Resources Center, 1970.

17. As in the case of air pollution, there is considerable controversy over what are permissible levels for each water pollutant.

18. For some representative figures of sewage generated, see S. Grava, *Urban Planning Aspects of Water Pollution Control*, New York and London, Columbia University Press, 1969, pp. 177-178.

19. Hydroscience, Inc., "*Simplified Mathematical Modeling of Water Quality*," Washington, D.C., Environmental Protection Agency, 1971.

*[Paragraphs in italics deal with retrospective analyses]*

## NOISE POLLUTION

### Measure 7. Change in noise and vibration levels, and the number of people bothered by excessive noise and vibration.

Developments may affect noise levels in the short term by construction, and in the long term by changes in vehicular and pedestrian traffic, industrial processes, and other activities.

Since noise increases will be most pronounced in the immediate vicinity of the development, measurement efforts should concentrate there. Usually the areawide effects will be diffuse, though in some circumstances they may be sharp enough to measure, as when a new shopping center draws so much traffic that noise levels rise all along corridors leading to it.

Individual developments rarely affect aircraft or railway noise in the short run,[20] though they can in the aggregate by stimulating increased population or business activity. However, present and potential aircraft and railway noise must be considered along with traffic and other noise in evaluating the suitability of a development for a site—especially for residential developments—in order to protect the future citizens and the community purse. A few years ago, the City of Los Angeles was required by the courts to purchase an entire residential area from the owners because noise from the nearby airport had become overwhelming.

### Data Collection for Past Development

*There are three basic approaches to assessing noise levels changes in the community: (1) Using simple, graphic noise assessment procedures such as those developed by the Department of Housing and Urban Development.*[21] *(2) Conducting physical measurements with a standard sound-level meter in the vicinity of the development site before and after development.*[22] *(3) Surveying a scientifically drawn sample of people in the community to determine their perceptions of changes in noise levels.*

*The first approach, which can be used for estimating the impacts of transportation-related noise from proposed as well as past developments, is based on the HUD Noise Assessment Guidelines.*[23] *It does not require actually measuring the noise but rather allows one to look up the expected noise levels on charts, given (a) the "effective distance" from the test point of interest to nearby roads, (b) the peak hourly automobile flow and (c) the peak hourly truck flow. The "effective distance" depends on the actual distance, the road gradient, the mean traffic speed, and the nature of sound barriers between the test point and the road. Four levels of noise acceptability are shown on the charts representing approximations to HUD noise criteria for the suitability of potential sites for new residential developments. However, although not developed for the purpose, they can also be used to estimate the nuisance of increased traffic to existing developments—the need here. Procedures for estimating railway and aircraft noise are also given.*

*The second approach, physical measurement, involves the collection of data using a standard A-weighted sound-level meter.*[24] *Raw data from this meter have been found to correlate quite well with human subjective responses—although not as well as some of the more sophisticated noise indexes.*[25]

*For possibly better correlations between physical measurements and human perceptions, sound meter data can be used to compute the Traffic Noise Index of Griffiths and Langdon*[26] *or the Noise Pollution Level developed by D.W. Robinson in 1969.*[27]

---

20. There are exceptions. For example, the introduction or expansion of a major dynamic enterprise to a small city can result in major changes in air traffic in a relatively short time.

21. See T.J. Schultz and N.M. McMahon, *Noise Assessment Guidelines*, prepared for the U.S. Department of Housing and Urban Development by Bolt, Beranek and Newman, Washington, D.C., Government Printing Office, 1972. The guidelines may have to be adjusted to represent varying sensitivities from community to community.

22. The absolute levels or computed indexes from them can be compared with criteria set by the Environmental Protection Agency, the Department of Housing and Urban Development, the Department of Labor, or others. As with air and water pollution, the effects of particular noise levels on human health and happiness is still unclear. For discussions of current standards, see for example, W.J. Galloway, W.E. Clark and J. Kerrick, *Highway Noise Simulation and Mixed Reaction*, Highway Research Board, Program Report No. 78, 1969; T.J. Schultz, *Noise Assessment Guidelines—Technical Background*, prepared for the Department of Housing and Urban Development by Bolt, Beranek and Newman, Washington, D.C., Government Printing Office, 1972; and Department of Housing and Urban Development, *Noise Abatement and Control: Department Policy, Implementation Responsibilities and Standards;* Circular No. 1309, 1971.

23. T.J. Schultz and N.M. McMahon, *Noise Assessment Guidelines*, op. cit.

24. People perceive different frequencies of sound and different sound pressure levels as different in loudness. "A-weighting" is a scheme that tries to reflect this by modifying the frequency response of a sound-level meter so that very low and very high frequency sounds count less toward loudness than midrange sounds.

25. Theodore J. Schultz, *Noise Assessment Guidelines—Technical Background*, op. cit. (in footnote 22 above). This reference also presents an excellent discussion and comparison of the various refined noise measures developed to date.

26. I.D. Griffiths and F.J. Langdon, "Subjective Responses to Road Traffic Noise," *Journal of Sound Vibrations*, Vol. 8, January 1968.

27. Edward A. Starr, "Measuring Noise Pollution," *Spectrum*, The Institute of Electrical and Electronics Engineers, Inc., Vol. 9, No. 6, June 1972, pp. 18-25. This article is an excellent summary of the problems and alternatives in measuring noise pollution.

*[Paragraphs in italics deal with retrospective analyses]*

*The Community Noise Exposure Level, which is part of California state codes regulating airports, can be used to rate the effects of noise from aircraft. It is a weighted sum of the hourly energy average of A-weighted sound levels. Different weightings are used for day, night, and evening.*

*For each of the above noise indexes, measurements should be made at various times of day and days of week at locations most likely to have increased noise and at points that are most representative of the majority of people in the vicinity. Measurements should be made before development starts, during construction, and after construction until activity in the development levels off. Several control points in the general neighborhood or similar neighborhoods should be measured before and after development to get some indication of how noise levels would have changed without the development. Care must be taken in choosing positions for making measurements with response to wind patterns, surrounding buildings, vegetation and so forth.*

*It would be desirable to collect sufficient data to prepare equal-noise-level contour maps that could be overlaid on population maps of the community. The number of people to be affected by a change in noise could then be computed.*

*Vibration measurements need not be made except in unusual circumstances. They are relatively expensive to do well and add little to simpler noise measurement. An exception might be for a development where significantly increased truck and bus traffic passes close to existing structures that may be damaged by the vibrations over the long run, or in which people are relatively sound-proofed but still are literally shaken. Unusual vibrations during construction process should likewise be considered.*

*The third approach to assessing the impact of development on noise levels is through the use of citizen surveys. Noise annoyance levels may vary considerably despite similar mechanical measurements of noise levels. Children yelling, buses, and music, for example, could all yield a similar sound meter reading but people might rate their annoyance quite differently. Because of this, surveys to determine the percent of people who are significantly annoyed or threatened by noise and vibrations added by the development are suggested. Allowance should be made for noise perceptions biased by individual attitudes toward the development.*

### Data Collection for Proposed Development

Noise *from* the existing community may have an impact *on* the proposed development and this can be evaluated using actual measurements or the HUD Noise Assessment Guidelines discussed above. Rough estimates of increases in road, railway, and air traffic for at least several years should be considered, but changing transportation technology may make such projections misleading if extended too far.

The impact caused *by* the proposed development on the existing community can be estimated in several ways:

- Use the HUD Noise Assessment Guidelines discussed above. Estimated changes in traffic on nearby streets and changes in nearby noise barriers can be used as input to the Guidelines to forecast whether the development would put certain neighborhoods or locations into worse categories of noise acceptability than before.

- Use analogous situations–similar developments built within the community or in comparable communities–to assess the likely change in noise levels. This is a crude approach but may give reasonably accurate guidance if several examples corresponding closely to the proposed development are examined.

- Perform a detailed analysis of expected noise and vibration sources (such as machinery) on the site, and traffic increases on or near the site. Noise from each type of source would be estimated as a function of time, and combined into a composite noise-generating profile. Expected noise levels at various points in the community could then be estimated, considering sound barriers and meterological conditions. Such an expensive, time-consuming approach is not usually necessary.

For proposed residential development and most commercial developments, where traffic is likely to be the most objectionable source of noise, the first method seems best. The third method will serve for sites where noise from machinery dominates and where residential or commercial uses are nearby. Where the first approach is too limited and the third too costly or complex, the second method may be used to get rough approximations. The second method also will serve as a good, common sense double-check on the others. Vibration estimates will only have to be made in exceptional situations, and will require special analysis.

## GREENERY AND OPEN SPACE

**Measure 8. Amount and percent change in greenery and open space.**

The amount of greenery and open space in a community is often directly changed by development. Greenery has significant economic, social, psychological, and aesthetic benefits: It can reduce pollution; save energy (via shade and wind screening); increase privacy; improve the climate in its immediate vicinity; and make life more pleasant. Open space affects aesthetics, recreation opportunity and the microclimate, and perceptions of crowdedness.

Many urban areas are trying to increase their amount of greenery and open space, or at least minimize losses. There is concern both for large, park-size tracts and for easy public access to smaller parks. Expanding suburbs are trying to preserve open space commensurate with expected growth.

At a minimum, estimates should be made of the **change in contiguous forested areas and green but unforested areas.*** Land with over 50 percent tree cover is considered forested. Other measurements might include **the percent and absolute change in greenery and usable open space on the development site,[28] and the absolute change in open space in community** (by whether private or public).[29] Greenery and open space are measured by area (square feet or acres, as appropriate) as viewed from above. For some situations communities might also note changes in the quality as well as the quantity of greenery.

These measures do not always adequately reflect the impact where the potential change in greenery and open space is small, as in a case where mature trees lining a road may be cut, or where a row of trees are to be added. An appropriate alternative measure for these cases is **the number of trees or plants to be lost or gained.**

Greenery and open space on the site before development can be quickly mapped if not already done so by the developer or it can be determined from available aerial photos of the site. The U.S. Department of Agriculture's Soil Conservation Service, the Interior Department's Geological Survey, and the National Aeronautic and Space Administration have aerial photos for many communities at various scales, dates, and color spectra. Local communities often have their own photos, as do developers, at least for the areas of their proposed developments. Greenery and open space planned for the development can be obtained from the site plan. Presenting photos and sketches of the scenery before and after development will often be a useful adjunct to the measures in describing changes in greenery and open space.

*Bold type emphasizes alternative impact measures that may be used instead of, or in addition to, the numbered measures from Exhibit 1 which appear before each section.

28. This includes greenery in front of buildings, in yards, and on roofs. Usable open space here is that unoccupied by streets, driveways, or parking space—it excludes balconies and includes unobstructed roof space that is safe and intended for recreational use. Even if these are small quantities they may be worth "measuring" to encourage attention to them.

29. This indicates the amount of space left, and is an indicator of the physical "openness" of the community—the opposite of "built-upness."

## WILDLIFE AND VEGETATION

**Measure 9. Number and types of rare or endangered species that will be threatened.**

**Measure 10. Change in the abundance and diversity of wildlife and vegetation in the development and community.**

Development may physically destroy vegetation and harm wildlife by altering or destroying habitats. The effects may be both on the site itself as a result of construction, and in the surroundings as a result of pollution from the development and secondary effects in the community.

The problem of rare species is not likely to be faced in most individual developments. But localized destruction of common species may significantly affect the quality of life in and near a development, and should not be ignored. Diversity of species is also thought to be an indicator of the stability (and thus the health) of the ecosystem.

*The impact of past development on wildlife and vegetation may be evaluated by site surveys before and after development to determine the diversity and abundance of major species at various times of the year. These surveys preferably should be made by professional zoologists, botanists, ecologists or other experts. Simple logs kept by onsite residents of numbers and species of wildlife observed might also be useful. For inventorying plant diversity, the populations within species, numbers of different species and their interspersion and spread over space should be noted. Changes in the abundance of nuisance species of wildlife and vegetation merit special attention. For major developments or series of developments, surveys ranging farther afield into neighboring lands and waters should be made to determine effects of pollution and loss of habitats.*

When estimating the impact of proposed development, the principal data collection technique could again be an inventory of existing wildlife and vegetation on the site to learn what may be endangered.

In the absence of an inventory, an analysis of habitat characteristics would provide a basis from which to make inferences. General characteristics to note include the number and types of plant communities (groups of plants usually found together), the linear amount of "edge" (such as the boundaries between woods and grasslands), the presence of water, and the presence of movement corridors between habitat areas. However, unless the site contains one of the few last habitats in the region for some species, it may be difficult to predict how the development will

*[Paragraphs in italics deal with retrospective analyses]*

affect the abundance of life forms in the area without special scientific studies. Effects of pollution on wildlife and vegetation also require special studies or analogies drawn from past examples.

As a surrogate measure where special studies are not feasible, the **percent of the local habitat that would be destroyed or adversely affected by the development** can be stated for major species found in the survey.

Many local communities cannot afford to retain the services of a trained scientist to collect data on wildlife and vegetation. Creation of advisory conservation communities, such as are often used in New England, may be a means of carrying out the task.

## SCARCE RESOURCE CONSUMPTION

### Measure 11. Change in the frequency, duration, and magnitude of shortages of critically scarce resources, and the number of persons affected.

The effect of new development on consumption of scarce resources, especially energy and fuels, is of increasing concern today.[30] Individual developments are unlikely to make a significant difference in local energy consumption, except where the development is very large or if shortages are very critical. Also, local energy problems tend to be overshadowed by regional and national energy policies. Nevertheless, new development collectively can influence local shortages. And at the minimum the efficiency of resource utilization can be estimated for individual developments. The discussion below is directed to electrical energy, natural gas, heating oil, and gasoline, but the general idea applies to any critically scarce resource, the shortage of which affects people's well-being and way of life.[31]

Evaluations should focus on the frequency, duration, and magnitude of shortages, that is, when demand exceeds supply. For example, the finding might be: "An expected additional two brownouts lasting up to three hours per year." This is intended as a proxy for the degree of inconvenience created. People generally will recognize how this would constrain or inconvenience them in terms of restricted use of television and other major appliances, but it might be desirable to explicitly describe the types of appliances, lights, etc., likely to be affected to bring the point home. Fuel oil shortages may be expressed in terms of temperature reductions.

30. A short summary of the energy problem and some potential solutions may be found in Gordon D. Friedlander, "Energy Conservation by Redesign," *IEEE Spectrum*, November 1973, pp. 36-43.

31. Of course, most resources are scarce. The emphasis should be on those few deemed most important.

If shortages get severe enough, it might be necessary to estimate their effects on health, such as the **expected changes in sickness or death rates due to insufficient heating.**

Energy shortages may also significantly affect employment, transportation, access to recreation, pollution, and so forth, and impact measures in these areas should take account of major changes in resource consumption.

In most cases, the direct, primary influences of a development, as in providing jobs, will overshadow the indirect, secondary effects resulting from potential resource shortages. Also, the secondary effects of energy shortages on jobs, transportation, etc., will be difficult to estimate without sophisticated models of the local economy and probably can be disregarded unless some obvious significant impact is apparent.

As in the case of pollution measures, energy impacts of most individual developments are likely to be too small to be significant. Cumulative effects of groups of developments need to be considered. Alternatively, for an individual development, the efficiency with which it uses energy resources might be estimated, in terms of **expected energy usage for heating and cooling in equivalent BTU's or KWH per square foot of usable interior space per year.** The degree to which the structure will conserve energy may be compared to local or national standards, or to local averages for recent developments of a similar nature.[32] Measuring efficiency may also be useful where the computation of energy shortages is too complex, such as when the local supply is subject to large unpredictable fluctuations.

Measuring the *change* in consumption as a result of development needs to take into account that some usage simply shifts within the community and does not materially affect overall consumption. For example, when a family or industrial plant relocates within the same community, the net change in consumption may go up or down, depending on whether it uses more or less energy after the move, and whether a comparable user moves in to fill its previous quarters. Also, usage per existing household or business may change over time and must be considered or forecast when estimating the likelihood of shortages.

Energy generated within a development itself, as in the case of an industry or apartment complex burning its solid waste to create power or heat, should be subtracted out of the requirements of the community.

### Electricity

For electrical energy consumption, the suggested measure for large developments or cumulative effects of

32. Friedlander, op. cit., states that if 75 percent of new housing units complied with recent FHA insulation standards, savings over the next decade would equal $24 \times 10^{11}$ KWH, which is more than the energy produced by present annual consumption of all fossil fuels.

development is the **expected number of brownouts (voltage reduction) or blackouts (no electricity) per year**, and the duration of the "out." For individual small developments, the efficiency measures previously cited might be used.

It would also be useful to translate voltage reductions into their more noticeable effects, such as whether lights would be dimmed or air conditioners unable to operate. Deliberate brownouts ordered as safety measures by the power company and accidential brownouts or blackouts should be distinguished.

*For assessing the impact of past developments, data on usage rates and incidents of shortfalls should be available from local utilities. Identifying the extent to which added consumption in a development caused or aggravated shortfalls will also require data on changes in usage for existing (predevelopment) units, changes in supply, and changes in energy allocation policies.*

Electrical energy requirements for proposed residential and commercial developments can be estimated from established local averages for analogous recent developments, or from design details of the development and assumptions about the behavior of the development's users. Adjustments can be made for anticipated energy-saving features such as extra heavy insulation, or for energy-wasting features such as glass walls. Estimates for industrial development depend on the nature and level of planned production, and data will probably be available from the industry itself.

The estimated electrical energy requirements, together with assumptions about changes in current customers' usage and the supply likely to be available to the community, can be used to estimate the potential for shortages. In many cases, the local power company can provide most of the needed data, if not the results themselves, since they too obviously must be concerned with potential shortages.

### Fuel Oil

Fuel oil is primarily used for heating. The effects of a development on allocating existing fuel oil supply might be expressed in terms of the **reduced home or office temperatures** that will be used as the basis for fuel allocation, and the **number of days that businesses or institutions are forced to close as a result of shortages.** Local field oil companies will be a major source of data, although the supplies are increasingly being managed on a regional, multistate basis. Here again, efficiency of usage rather than impact in shortages should be used for small, individual developments.

### Natural Gas

Because of the character and distribution of gas, supplies cannot readily be rationed to particular customers or delivered in reduced amounts to all customers as in electric power brownouts. Thus, unless ample future supplies are reasonably assured, the gas utility itself may withhold gas altogether from new development. If gas is to be used, one would try to measure the resulting **number of existing customers required to switch to another fuel** or the **average change in home temperatures due to short supplies.** In any case, the measure used should be adapted to reflect the allocation procedures used locally, and efficiency measures used for evaluating small developments.

### Gasoline

Because gasoline is allocated at community-wide, regional, and national levels, localized shortages usually will not be computable or even make sense to consider for particular developments and possibly even groups of developments. But individual developments do influence demand by the degree to which they affect the numbers and lengths of private vehicular trips. Thus the change in the **number of car-miles per capita** to be required by the development relative to per capita usage in the rest of the community, and the **number of persons in the development within walking distance of everyday shopping needs or other facilities** might be used as surrogate measures of the efficiency of resource utilization. However, such measures may not clearly reflect whether a development's location will lead to excessive gasoline consumption, especially in communities with much room to grow. What might appear an inefficient location in the short term might prove efficient in the long term as the area develops. For example, the first phase of a new development far from food and other stores may not seem optimally located, but the location of the stores may be optimum once the entire development is completed.

## NATURAL DISASTERS

### Measure 12. Change in number of people and value of property endangered by flooding, earthquakes, landslides, mudslides, and other natural disasters.

Natural disasters take a large toll in life and property each year, and cost large sums of public money. Yet much construction goes on in danger zones in the path of these disasters—sometimes from ignorance, sometimes from greed, and sometimes because community needs are deemed worth the risks.

In evaluating a change in land use, the risks from floods, earthquakes, landslides, mudslides, hurricanes, tornadoes, land subsidence over abandoned mines, volcanoes, and other natural disasters should be explicitly stated in terms of the property value and the number of people

*EXHIBIT 6*

## FORMAT FOR PRESENTING THE EFFECT OF A DEVELOPMENT ON RISKS FROM NATURAL DISASTERS

| Type of Disaster | Additional People Jeopardized | | Additional Property Value Jeopardized | |
|---|---|---|---|---|
| | Within Development | Outside Development | Within Development | Outside Development |
| | | | (millions of dollars) | |
| *Floods* | | | | |
| Worst in 10 years | 1,000 | 0 | $10 | 0 |
| Worst in 50 years | 3,000 | 100 | $40 | $.5 |
| Worst in 100 years | 3,000 | 100 | $40 | $.5 |
| *Earthquakes* | | | | |
| Worst in 10 years | 0 | 0 | 0 | 0 |
| Worst in 50 years | 500 | 0 | $5 | 0 |
| Worst in 100 years | 1,000 | 0 | $15 | 0 |

**NOTES:**
1. The zero entries do not mean that there would be no damage, but rather that there would be no *added* jeopardy as a result of the proposed development.
2. If historic experience is not available, other measures of seriousness may be relied on.

whose residences and places of work will be jeopardized. The people and property at risk should be indicated for disasters with various probabilities of occurence, such as the risk from the worst flood expected every five years, every ten years, every 50 years, etc.

A new development also might increase the hazards to the rest of the community. By removing natural barriers, changing land contours, and contributing to changes in vegetation and soil permeability, for example, a new development can expose previously safe parts of the community to flood dangers. One development may not significantly affect land cover, but a series may. Cumulative impacts and trends, as well as immediate changes, are crucial.

A development can add to community safety by reversing or reducing previous hazards. For example, it may allow people to relocate their homes or businesses to safer grounds, or it may provide emergency shelter.

The types of disasters to consider vary greatly from one jurisdiction to another. Also, high levels of risk may apply to the entire jurisdiction or to only the part left for growth. If there can be no expansion without risk, this must be explicitly weighed against the need for residences and economic growth.

The number of people and value of property jeopardized can vary according to public and private protective actions, such as construction of dams. These factors should be considered in the data collection and analysis.

An illustration of data presentation to assess disaster impacts is shown in Exhibit 6.

*In evaluating the impacts of a past development on the harm from natural disasters, previous disasters both before and after development should be studied to determine the extent of damage and the number of people affected to see whether the changed land use made any difference. Usually there will be few if any disasters to analyze, in which case the evaluation would be similar to that for proposed developments.*

In evaluating the impact of a proposed development, a number of published data sources can be used. For many regions, maps exist showing the flood plains at different intensities of flooding.[33] These maps and related information, coupled with the plans for building locations, heights, terrain reconfiguration, construction materials, and planned defensive measures, can be used to estimate the number of people and value of property jeopardized. This is generally more feasible to do for hazards to the new development than for its effects on the existing community. The effects of changes in land cover and storm drainage on flood severity and frequency in the existing community can be estimated using hydrologic (discharge) models incorporating land cover variables. These models have to be tailored to each community.[34]

The National Seismic Risk Map of the United States[35] can be used to determine whether a community is in a high risk area for damage from tremors or earthquakes. A variety of more detailed maps are available or under development for some areas; they show where landslides have occurred in the past and where geologic fault lines lie.[36] Most areas do not yet have detailed risk maps. If they are designated as high hazard regions on the national map, they should be analyzed for risk by the local jurisdiction's engineers or expert consultants.

Knowledge of construction materials and techniques for the new development and local meterological conditions can be used to assess risk from wind, hurricanes, and other meterological conditions. Special studies should be made to assess dangers from other natural disasters.

---

33. Care must be taken to see how the flood plain is defined on such maps. A variety of definitions have been used. For an expanded discussion, see Michael P. Greenberg and Robert M. Hordon, "Environmental Impact Statements and Some Annoying Questions," *AIP Journal,* May 1974, pp. 164-75. (This includes an excellent discussion on water-related impact measurement problems, too.)

34. For a discussion of techniques and guidelines for assessing impact of land cover and storm drainage, see S.E. Rantz, "Suggested Criteria for Hydrologic Design of Storm-Drainage Facilities in the San Francisco Bay Region, California," San Francisco Bay Region Environment and Resources Planning Study, 1972. One well documented example of a particularized model is Tennessee Valley Authority, *Upper Bear Creek Experimental Project, A Continuous Daily Stream Flow Model,* TVA, Division of Water Control Planning, 1972. Also, Ben Chie Yen, "Methodologies for Flow Prediction in Urban Storm Drainage Systems," Department of Civil Engineering, University of Illinois, Champaign-Urbana, 1973.

35. National Seismic Risk Map, U.S. Department of Commerce, Environmental Science Services Administration, Coast and Geodetic Survey, circa 1969.

36. See, for example, T.H. Nilsen, "Preliminary Photo-interpretation Map of Landslide and Other Surficial Deposits of the Mount Diablo Area, Contra Costa and Alameda Counties, California," 1971; F.A. Taylor and E.E. Brabb, "Map Showing Distribution and Cost by Counties of Structurally Damaging Landslides in the San Francisco Bay Region, California, Winter of 1968-69," 1972; and R.D. Brown and E.W. Wolfe, "Map Showing Recently Active Breaks Along the San Andreas Fault Between Point Delgada and Bolinos Bay, California," 1970, all part of the San Francisco Bay Region Environment and Resources Planning Study, U.S. Department of Housing and Urban Development and U.S. Department of the Interior.

# III. AESTHETICS AND CULTURAL VALUES

This set of measures attempts to reflect the impact of development on aesthetic and cultural concerns of the citizenry–especially changes in the physical attractiveness and landmarks of the community–which play important roles in the enjoyment of life, community pride, psychological stress, and land values. But whether they are measurable, how to measure them, and the degree of responsibility which local government should assume for them are less certain–in part because the issues have been neglected.

Most people consider the following negative elements as detracting from aesthetic enjoyment (the pertinent measures are cited in parentheses): blocked views (13), bad odors (5), smoke in the air (5), dirty water (6), and noise (7).

Positive elements of physical attractiveness vary with tastes. The amount of greenery and open space (8) seems significant to many. Other positive elements include wildlife and flora (9), local landmarks (16), and the existence of "views" (13). However, it is easily recognized that intangible qualities of design, the balance of structures and space, and the type of greenery can all add to or detract from what makes an attractive neighborhood, aside from or in addition to any specific measure. For this reason, it is suggested that Measures 14 and 15 be used to indicate citizen perceptions of the overall aesthetic effect.

## VIEWS

### Measure 13. Number of people whose views or sightlines are blocked, degraded, or improved.

A new development may interfere with people's views of the scenery or remove obstructions. A new tall building, for example, may block the view of green space from an existing building. Razing buildings to create a plaza may open up previously blocked views.

The number of people whose views will become wholly or partially blocked, and the number of people who will gain an improved view through the removal of obstructions should be estimated. The sightlines blocked by the development and the nature of the old and new vistas can be determined geometrically from plans, maps and photos, and by site visits.[1]

For landscapes and cityscapes that are considered unusually attractive, added data describing loss or gain of views might be desired. The nature of the view might best be conveyed using photos or sketches. The fraction of present views that become obscured can also be noted. Loss of a particularly attractive part of the view–a waterfall, stream, or garden–might be counted as a "major obscuration" even if it represents only a small percentage of the scene. However, a new development should not be scored poorly if the panorama in question is already blocked by previous buildings.

Distinctions might be made between sightline changes for residential and nonresidential buildings, when it is assumed the occupants will place different values on them. Certain businesses and tourist attractions are dependent on their views, and harm to them should be specifically noted.

Estimating the numbers of people whose views will be blocked is not easy. Should passersby be included? Do you count "windows" or do you count "people" whose views are obscured?

---

1. For a good description of view protection and regulatory devices, see the American Society of Planning Officials, *View Protection Regulations*, Report No. 213, 1966.

For private residences other than highrises, all occupants might be counted. For highrises and business establishments, the approximate number of the occupants or daily users whose views will be affected might be noted. People affected can be roughly estimated using the average number of occupants per type of housing unit, times the number of housing units, or by using census or other population sources. For commercial areas, it is suggested that diagrams be drawn to show the areas from which views are obscured, including public areas such as streets. The number of people affected can then be roughly estimated.

## ATTRACTIVENESS

### Measure 14. Visual attractiveness of the development as rated by citizens and "experts."

### Measure 15. Percent of citizens who think the development improves or lessens overall neighborhood attractiveness, pleasantness, and uniqueness.

One of the longest lasting impacts of a development is its effect on community attractiveness. Attractiveness affects people's attitudes toward their community, which in turn affects property values and the desirability of the community for future growth and investment.

The numerous factors relevant to daytime visual attractiveness include colors, textures, patterns, and relation of buildings to each other and to the terrain.[2] However, it is the overall effect, including the movement of the people and vehicles, that counts. Thus, data describing or rating the various design elements are of questionable value for impact assessment (though possibly useful for suggesting corrective actions).

Some may find a new development physically attractive, but still prefer the original appearance of the neighborhood for its character, image, relation to personal identity, or familiarity. For this reason a second measure of attractiveness (15) has been introduced. The two may be correlated, since overall attitudes expressed in Measure 15 may color perceptions of the physical appearance expressed in Measure 14. Without further research to confirm this, however, the two perspectives of 14 and 15 probably should be considered separately.

Citizen surveys seem to be one of the few systematic approaches for estimating perceptions of attractiveness, since models for estimating aesthetic preferences are lacking.[3]

### Data Collection for Past Development

*People who live or work in close proximity to the development in question will usually be the most important group to survey. Other people within sight of the development and people in the general community might be surveyed as well, focusing on broader impressions of the development's contribution to or detraction from the townscape or landscape. Opinions of architects, art critics, artists, urban planners and other professionals might also be sought, especially for developments that are large or that will attract widespread attention and use, such as recreation or cultural centers.*[4]

*To ensure that each person surveyed knows what the development under study looks like, photos from several viewpoints or in-person visits may be used. The presentation media should be consistent for all those surveyed. Each person should then be asked to rate the attractiveness of the development and of the previous use of the site (if he had firsthand knowledge of it). Specific reasons for disliking or liking a development might be asked to determine, for example, whether the general style, specific design, the structures themselves, or neighborhood compatibility were decisive factors.*

*Surveys of aesthetic judgments present a number of problems. Opinions on attractiveness itself may be substantially modified by other aspects or beliefs about a development, such as its cost, its impact on jobs, the activities or people displaced, and the people it attracts.*[5] *A related problem is that it may be difficult to separate one's sentimental feelings for one's old neighborhood from the "pure" appearance of the new development, even when the latter may appear more attractive or "pretty" to observers without any involvement.*

*A variety of more sophisticated techniques might be*

2. Nightime attractiveness might also be considered in appropriate circumstances.

3. Whether surveys will give the same or different data on perceptions than may be obtained at public hearings will be of great interest to test. This applies to all perception measures, not just those on aesthetics. For two interesting but not yet operationally satisfactory alternatives to surveys, see L.E. Shafer, Jr., J.F. Hamilton, Jr., and E.A. Schmidt, "Natural Landscape Preferences: A Predictive Model," *Journal of Leisure Research*, Vol. 29, No. 173, April 1970, pp. 1-19, and L.B. Leopold, "Landscape Esthetics," *Ekistics*, Vol. 29, No. 173, April 1970, pp. 271-77.

4. For a description of an experiment to determine the degree of agreement among art experts and between experts and laymen on the aesthetic merits of paintings, see J.W. Getzels, and M. Csikszentmiltalyi, "Aesthetic Opinion: An Emperical Study," prepared for the U.S. Department of Health, Education and Welfare, Cooperative Research Project 5-080, University of Chicago, 1965. It was found that artists agree to only a moderate though statistically significant extent among themselves, and that agreement between art experts and laymen ranged from fair to poor.

5. For elaboration of this point, see J.M. Fitch, "Experimental Bases for Esthetic Decisions," in H.M. Proshansky, W.H. Ittelson and L.G. Rivlin, eds., *Environmental Psychology*, New York, Holt, Rinehart and Winston, pp. 76-84.

*used to ascertain aesthetic opinions.*[6] *But it is unclear whether the added difficulties and expense generally are justified. Instead, questions are suggested that will reflect (1) the perceived physical attractiveness and (2) whether the citizens feel the new development has increased or decreased the attractiveness or uniqueness of the neighborhood. Considering the new land use alone, and then comparing it with the former use, would permit a finding, for example, that "the new development is rated very attractive by most citizens, but they prefer the way the neighborhood looked before." The data obtained from the aesthetics survey questions should be viewed in light of other perceptions–about crowdedness, noise, traffic hazard, privacy, friendliness, and overall satisfaction.*

*It should be remembered that people tend to adapt to their environment; once a new development has been around, people grow accustomed to its face. The retrospective evaluation may be quite different from the prospective one for the same development. Analysis drawn from retrospective evaluations for making decisions on proposed developments thus has many risks.*

### Data Collection for Proposed Development

Evaluating the aesthetic appeal of a proposed development can also be attempted using survey techniques, but this poses two major additional problems: how to convey an accurate impression of what the development would look like, and how to correct for the widely varying amounts of hearsay information and prejudices about the proposal that different citizens will have built up at the time they are interviewed.

Common devices for representing the development site and its surroundings are architectural plans, artists' sketches, aerial and street level photos with the development drawn in, and three-dimensional scale models. The relation between a person's evaluation after exposure to a photo or model and the same person's evaluation after firsthand experience has not yet been experimentally determined.[7] Therefore, records should be kept of which presentation modes were used and what background material was presented.

To help offset possible distortions from prejudices, the survey should be conducted early in the review process and each person surveyed should be given the same basic information about the development. Identifying the reasons for dissatisfaction, if any, may provide clues as to whether the aesthetic opinion is based on physical appearances or on other factors.

## LANDMARKS

### Measure 16. Rarity and perceived importance of cultural, historic, or scientific landmarks to be lost or made inaccessible.

Developments may destroy, impair access to, or crowd landmarks such as architecturally important buildings and archeological sites. The importance of landmarks within a community should be rated (at least qualitatively) in terms of rarity, distance to closest similar example, interest to tourists and the public, and interest to scholars. Sources for the necessary data include scholars in the appropriate discipline, the literature of the field, lists of official landmarks, historic preservation groups and citizen surveys.

*Rarity* may be expressed as the number of existing examples essentially equivalent to the threatened landmark. For example, a particular archeological earthworks might be described as one out of 100 known examples of its kind, and one out of three of its size. An architectural landmark might be described as one of the three multistory buildings by a famed architect, and the last with certain features representative of its period.

*Distance to closest similar example* may be expressed in miles or travel time to indicate the degree to which removing the landmark would curtail opportunity for enjoyment or learning.

*Importance or interest to the public* has often been neglected but should be taken into account. The percent of the public feeling a landmark is worth saving can be obtained by a survey of citizens. A small random telephone survey of as few as 30 to 50 respondents would probably suffice in most cases to estimate the intensity of feelings about whether to save–or remove–the landmark in question. A simple query could categorize a landmark as "a must to save," "important to save," "nice, but not important," "don't care," or "an unpleasant feature that should be removed."[8]

*Tourist usage and enjoyment* may be expressed in two ways, (1) as annual attendance figures, and (2) as subjective ratings based on attention in domestic and foreign guidebooks, queries to travel agents, and surveys of tourists visiting the landmark. The rating scale could be

6. These include adjective checklists, the Gough adjective checklist, activity and mood checklists, and semantic differentials tests. In these methods, rather than being asked for a single overall impression, the interviewee would be asked to check off which adjectives best described the development from a list he is given, or he chooses where the development lies between the pairs of adjectives such as beautiful-ugly, gay-sad, and cheerful-depressing.

7. Kenneth H. Craik, "The Comprehension of the Everyday Environment," *Environmental Psychology*, op. cit., pp. 646-658.

8. Most developments will not interfere with landmarks, and this survey will be infrequently needed. Also, survey questions could be part of one integrated questionnaire used to obtain data simultaneously for several measures of perceptions.

*[Paragraphs in italics deal with retrospective analyses]*

similar to that used in the Michelin tourist guides–zero to three stars, corresponding to ordinary, somewhat interesting, worth a detour, and worth a journey. Local officials also should refer to listings in the National Register (established as part of the 1966 Historic Preservation Act) for sites, buildings, and objects of national significance to American history, architecture, archeology, and culture, and to similar local or state registers.

*Importance to scholarly disciplines*–how critical a landmark is for research or teaching–may be determined by seeking opinions from historians, artists, scientists, and members of architectural and historical review boards.

# IV. PUBLIC AND PRIVATE SERVICES

This section deals with measuring impacts of development on the quality of the traditional major line services provided by local government–water, public health, crime control, fire protection, recreation, education, and transportation. Effects on some other line services, such as pollution control and storm drainage, are included in Measures 5-12 dealing with the natural environment.

Developments affect demand for services and the environment in which they are provided and thereby the quality of services. Although government interest is mainly centered on public services, it should consider development impacts on the quality and quantity of some private services as well, since there is much interaction between the two. For example, the addition or removal of private swimming pools may affect the crowdedness of public facilities. Therefore, it makes sense to measure the impact of development according to functions or types of services, whether provided by public or private sources.

The degree to which services are affected by development is closely tied to the predevelopment quality of service, the resulting changes in public spending, and the remaining capacity of existing facilities. Fiscal impact estimates, as noted earlier, may not reflect localized or short-term changes in service quality. Fiscal studies are often based on the presumption that the existing level of service will be maintained, whereas in reality construction of facilities or budget outlays may lag behind need. The studies frequently assume that per capita costs of maintaining service quality will remain constant, failing to account for rising costs.

The fiscal study alone may not point out particular service problems that may arise even though overall spending levels and facility plans seem satisfactory on the surface. Thus both the fiscal impacts and actual service impacts need to be measured to describe the tradeoffs between the two and how each dimension may change over time.

Because most large jurisdictions and many small ones have building and health codes and other legal provisions to regulate new developments, measures of structural safety and public health impacts are not included in the measures in this report. The codes, however, generally are minimum standards, and there may be large variations in risk even from hazards they protect against.

For example, flood hazards vary depending on where buildings are located and how they are constructed. Fire hazards vary with the building materials used, their furnishings, architectural details, and whether windows can be opened, even if there are no code violations. Thus there is need for evaluating the effects of a development on at least some aspects of public safety and health even if it complies with all existing codes and ordinances.

Finally, it may appear strange to see measures of shopping included with considerations of public services. Yet local government does affect shopping opportunities. Government, for instance, designates areas to be used for commercial enterprises through master planning and zoning. So it is appropriate to consider how proposed development will affect accessibility and other aspects of shopping.

## DRINKING WATER

**Measure 17. Change in the rate of water shortage incidents.**

**Measure 18. Change in indexes of drinking water quality and safety.**

Development may affect water quality by polluting surface and ground water sources or by increasing demand so that supplies must be drawn from inferior sources. In either case, drinking water may be made safe, but purification processing may affect aesthetic qualities and raise water costs. Added demand from development may also occasionally cause shortages, necessitating rationing of water for bathing and watering lawns, or even for drinking.

New development might also lead communities to utilize modern water purification and reclamation technology, such as recycling of water, which might improve quality and quantity possibly even at lower costs.[9] (However, it is more likely that unit costs will increase, which should be considered in cost/revenue analysis.)

Except for a very large development relative to community size, no single land use proposal is likely to cause significant changes in drinking water. However, a series of developments may.

### Data Collection for Past Development

*The frequency and duration of incidents of water shortage in the community before and after development can be obtained from the records of the city manager or mayor's office, the water engineer, by citizen survey, and from newspaper files about requests for voluntary cutbacks in water use. Also, many fire departments monitor and record water pressure changes to ensure they meet fire-fighting requirements.*

*Health officials regularly sample water to determine bacteriological and chemical impurities, taste, odor, and turbidity.*[10] *Sample records before and after development should be compared. Citizen surveys can determine changes in how much water people drink and their opinion of the water's taste, odor, and appearance. Surveys are especially useful in instances where the aesthetic factors change, or where water quality becomes a public issue.*

*The basic problem in analyzing data will be isolating the changes due to development. If the development requires new purification techniques or if new kinds of effluents are added, direct effects will be more apparent. Usually the development simply adds to existing problems, so its incremental effects must be separated from water quality changes due to general community growth.*

9. New technologies are being tried in Lake Tahoe and Colorado Springs. See "Wastewater Treatment Processes and the Creation of Reclaimed Water as a Commercial Product," Second Urban Technology Conference, San Francisco, 1972, AIAA, New York.

10. For water quality standards, see U.S. Department of Health, Education, and Welfare, *Public Health Service Drinking Water Standards*, Revised, Washington, D.C., 1962. Standards are controversial for some types of pollutants, especially with regard to long-range effects on humans.

### Data Collection for Proposed Development

Projecting whether there will be water shortages can be based on known usage rates for various business and household characteristics applied to the development plans. Projected usage by the development would be compared to available supplies, expected rainfall, and general use trends. Proper planning usually can preclude water shortages, although occasional lags in facility capacity may occur.

Expected change in water quality can also be predicted under some circumstances. For example, the expected characteristics of water after treatment with new processing techniques can be provided by water engineers. They should indicate whether **water quality changes are likely to be noticeable or objectionable by none, some, or most of the community**. If hazardous pollutants will be increased, it is important to estimate how close these will approach safety limits.

## HOSPITAL CARE

**Measure 19. Change in number of citizens who are beyond x minutes travel time from a hospital emergency room (using such time as the community considers reasonable).**

**Measure 20. Change in average number of days of waiting time for hospital admittance for elective surgery.**

The main effect of most developments on the quality of local hospital care will be on the crowdedness of existing facilities and the accessibility of existing facilities to both the newcomers and the existing residents. Large developments or cumulative demand from developments may also stimulate construction of new hospitals, which may improve the quality of hospital services available to the existing community, as well as uncrowdedness and accessibility.

The location of a development with respect to nearby hospitals and local traffic conditions affect the travel time to reach an emergency room from the development. Needless to say this may be a life or death issue. If the development changes local traffic conditions, the travel time for persons in the surrounding community may be affected as well. If people in the community (other than those in the development) are not affected, the measure might be restated as **average travel time for a person in the development to reach an emergency room.**

Average waiting time in days for admission to a hospital for elective surgery is an indicator of the crowdedness of local hospitals. Waiting time may also be affected by factors such as community health conditions, admission policy, health insurance, personal income, and doctors'

*[Paragraphs in italics deal with retrospective analyses]*

policies about hospitalization. These may overshadow changes as a result of development.

### Data Collection for Past Development

*The percent of people within x minutes of emergency rooms can be computed using a map showing location of hospitals with emergency rooms and the population distribution of the community. Travel time will vary by time of day because of traffic conditions. Peak and off-peak times, or the time of day when most emergencies occur, should be considered.*

*The average waiting time for admission and the percent of capacity may be obtained from hospital records or possibly from a survey of doctors using nearby hospitals. If overcrowding exists, data on average stays, changes in hospital or doctors' policies, and the percent of patients coming from areas of new development should be collected to help determine if it is due to new development or to increased usage by the existing community.*

### Data Collection for Proposed Development

Estimates of travel times should take account of the location of new hospitals to be built and expected changes in traffic computed for the transportation measurements. Expected changes in waiting times can be computed by assuming some frequency and duration of hospital visits based on local experience with people with socioeconomic characteristics similar to those of the incoming population, or more simply, based on current per person usage in the community. Preferably, trends in per person usage should be considered, and not just usage at a point in time. A major problem in estimating crowdedness for individual hospitals is that people tend to go to hospitals associated with their doctors, or reported to be especially good for the service they seek, and not just to the nearest hospital. Unless there is a regional hospital shortage, or usage models developed for the region, it may be difficult to estimate waiting times for specific hospitals.

## CRIME CONTROL

**Measure 21. Change in rate of crimes in existing community or new development (or expert rating of change in hazard presented).**

**Measure 22. Change in percent of people feeling a lack of security from crime.**

Potential changes in crime rates[11] and perceived crime hazards are a prime issue in many rezoning evaluations, especially in residential areas. Developments may affect crime rates in a community by adding or removing targets (people, businesses, residences) and by changing physical or social conditions that may breed crime or make it easier to commit crimes.

The potential targets for economic crime may change in number, density, vulnerability, or lucrativeness. For example, a new office building may increase the opportunities for larceny. Crime attracted by the development may spill over into the existing community or the development might attract crime away from the existing community. Either way, whether there is a net change in crime is a complex issue. It is partially a function of how well the existing community is known and being "worked" by criminals, and of relative conditions in the new and old areas. The vulnerability of the new development can be decreased by such factors as lighting, guards, surveillance systems, clear fields of view, and pedestrian activity after dark; it can be increased by ease of building entry, and unattended out-of-sight stairs, hallways, and basements.[12]

As examples of the affect of socioeconomic factors on crime rates, economic crimes may be reduced if the development reduces unemployment rates, while vandalism, car thefts, and narcotic offenses might be expected to increase if the teenage population increases.

The ability of police to deter crime might be affected by development. Increases in noncrime duties, such as traffic control, may reduce the time available for patrol duties. The size of the force may not increase fast enough to keep up with the new growth. People in the new community may not cooperate as willingly with police on crime prevention or detection. And response time to crime calls may be increased because of increased traffic congestion.

How people perceive their safety is as important to them as actual crime rates. Therefore, the degree to which citizen feelings of security are affected in the neighborhood of the development should be estimated.

### Data Collection for Past Development

*The most recognizable crime impacts are likely to be in the immediate neighborhood of the development. Crime rates by type of crime should, therefore, be determined for the periods before, during and after development in the police district containing the development, and in the adjacent districts.*

---

11. *Crime rate* here signifies the number of crimes against residents per 100 residents per year and the number of crimes against businesses per 100 businesses per year, and not just the absolute total of crimes per year.

12. For interesting discussions on how urban design might affect crime, see Oscar Newman, *Defensible Space: Crime Prevention through Urban Design*, New York, Macmillan, 1972; and S. Angel, "Discouraging Crime through City Planning," University of California, Institute of Urban and Regional Development, Working Paper No. 75, 1968.

*Crime rates for the areas outside and within the development should be estimated separately to distinguish between effects of development on the existing community and on people in the development. The new development might have a high crime rate and affect the overall community crime rate without increasing the rate of crimes against those outside the development.*

*Change in crime rates in the neighborhood with the development should be compared to changes in comparable neighborhoods used as controls to determine if the changes may reasonably be attributed to factors in the development under consideration.*

*The crime categories for which rates should be compared include those in the FBI crime index (murder, rape, assault, robbery, larceny, auto theft), serious narcotic crimes, and vandalism, and any other crimes of particular concern to the community. Data on index crimes are collected by most jurisdictions by month and year. Data on other crimes, and data on crimes by police district, neighborhood, or precinct also are often available. Some police departments keep track of where crimes occur with pins on a map, simplifying data collection for specific neighborhoods.*

*It is important to remember that available police data usually refer to* **reported** *crimes, not total crimes committed. A new development may change the percent of crimes that are reported in some crime categories, perhaps as a result of improved or worsened police-community relations. Total crime can be estimated from victimization surveys (interviews to determine the actual number of crimes that occurred whether reported to the police or not). Unfortunately, unless a victimization survey is made within the development, the usual citywide surveys probably will not contain a large enough sample of persons in the development to distinguish between the degree of underreporting within and outside the development. However, a major change in underreporting in the part of the city containing the development may be detectable from the general surveys. A special victimization survey for the development might be coupled with survey questions for other measures in a multipurpose survey to aid in assessing impacts of development.*

*The number of persons living in the development who were arrested for crimes in the community might be another indicator of how the development contributed to crime patterns. Comparable data from the previous land use should also be collected so the before-and-after differences can be fairly analyzed.*

*Data for the second suggested measure, the change in the percent of people feeling a lack of security from crime, can be obtained from citizen surveys conducted before and after development. The second survey might ask about changes in the feeling of security over the time period from before to after development and the reasons for any changes, to learn if they are related to the new development. There has been considerable experience under LEAA sponsorship of surveys that attempt to gauge feelings of security. Typical questions ask whether the person feels safe walking alone in the neighborhood at night and in daytime.*

## Data Collection for Proposed Development

For most new developments it will not be possible to make reliable estimates of their impact on crime. Knowledge about the quantitative relationship between crime rates and the causes of crime is limited, and wholly satisfactory methods of predicting crime rates do not exist. Crude approaches, however, might be tried on the premise that an educated guess is usually better than pure conjecture.

Crime rates in the new development can be roughly estimated based on knowledge of an area's current crime rates and trends by type of business or residence. For example, Detroit keeps data on the number of burglaries and larcenies by type of business (e.g., department stores, groceries, etc.) and type of residence (e.g., single-family residences, apartments).[13] These data can be applied to the number of establishments or units of each type in the development plan.

A second approach is to draw analogies from previous experience with similar developments in similar neighborhoods. The detailed design of the buildings, open space, lighting, types of activity by time of day, etc., should be considered, not just the general land use. If, in spite of variations in certain details that will almost always exist, a particular type of development in a particular kind of neighborhood usually resulted in a significant crime increase, it would be reasonable to expect a similar result in like circumstances. The estimated change might then be stated in qualitative terms such as the **likelihood of major increase, minor increase, or no significant change**. On the other hand, if case histories show vast differences in crime rate effects for developments similar in gross characteristics, one would have to conclude that wide variations could result, stating frankly that the elements which cause high or low crime impacts have not yet been identified, and that estimates either way are unreliable.

The gross analogy approach has the advantage of treating the totality of changes, indicating impact on the surrounding community and not just on the development site itself. In addition, it might give an indication of how feelings of security might change. But it must be considered a speculative approach until there has been an opportunity to subject it to considerable further testing.

---

13. Detroit Police Department, *1971 Annual Report*.

*[Paragraphs in italics deal with retrospective analyses]*

## FIRE PROTECTION

### Measure 23. Change in fire incidence rates.

### Measure 24. Change in rating of fire spread and rescue hazards.

Fire hazards are infrequently mentioned in land development evaluations. This is partly a tribute to the success of building code enforcement and modern fire departments in preventing fires and keeping them from spreading. But it seems also to stem from an under-appreciation of the hazards that remain. For example, in many modern buildings serious hazards may persist from (1) the smoke of even small fires because their windows cannot be opened, (2) materials that give off toxic fumes when ignited, and (3) the difficulties in escaping, especially from highrise structures.

Fire hazard from new developments may be considered in two parts: the change in the likelihood of a fire getting started in the first place, as measured by fire rates, and the change in the likely spread and risk to life of fire once started. The issue goes beyond risks to occupants of the new development; it concerns other members of the community who may visit, work, or shop there; it involves the potential spread of fire to the rest of the community; it may mean added risks for firemen; and it may increase fire protection costs generally.

Fire incidence may be affected by many aspects of new development:

- Types of construction and materials.
- Equipment, processes, and activities in the development.
- Education level, age distribution, and attitudes of new entrants into the community (which have a bearing on arson, false alarms, and accidental fires).
- Character of previous development (removal of blighted buildings, for instance, would probably reduce fire hazards).

Fire spread may be affected by the above factors, and others:

- Overall design, street layout, and proximity of buildings to each other.
- Hydrant locations and built-in private fire defenses.
- Distance to nearest fire station.
- Adequacy of amount and type of firefighting equipment and personnel in light of the needs of the new development, such as special fire towers for highrise buildings.

Note that development may lead to improved fire suppression for the community by providing enough concentration to warrant additional fire houses, fire personnel, and special equipment that will be available most of the time for standby protection to the rest of the community.

### Data Collection for Past Development

*Most communities keep fire records that can be used for estimating the impact of past development on fire incidence. These records permit fire incidence rates to be determined by type of building structure, and by type of business or residence. Data on the extent of damage and spread of fires for various structures, though less commonly used than incidence rates, can also be collected.*[14] *Arson or false alarms attributable to residents or others associated with the old and new land use might be compiled from police and fire department records. Changes in fire insurance ratings, if any, would give further clues for assessing the hazard from new development.*

### Data Collection for Proposed Development

Expected fire incident rates can be estimated from the community's past experience by type of structure or kind of business or industry. When there are few or no buildings or situations comparable to the expected developments, the data might have to be supplemented by information from nearby or similar communities. Rates for residences should preferably be further subdivided by demographic and socioeconomic characteristics, although this kind of breakdown is not yet available in most jurisdictions.

Because it is probably not possible with the current state-of-the-art of fire protection to quantitatively describe the probability of a certain degree of spread, damage or injuries, we suggest using a qualitative rating as to the risk of fire spreading from the new development to the rest of the community, noting any special problems that might hinder or increase the danger of firefighting and rescue operations. The rating would be based on expert opinions from fire engineers or the fire department as to the change in hazard level to the community, taking into account changes in the fire department as well as the plans for the proposed development. Any anticipated change in fire

14. A method for measuring fire spread is discussed in P.S. Schaenman and J. Swartz, *Measuring Fire Protection Productivity in Local Government–Some Initial Thoughts*, National Fire Protection Association, Boston, 1974.

insurance ratings as a result of equipment changes or other factors should be explicitly stated.

## RECREATION

**Measure 25. Change in the number of people within—or beyond—a reasonable distance (x miles or y minutes) from recreational facilities, by type of facility.**

**Measure 26. Change in usage as a percent of capacity; waiting times; number of people turned away; facility space per resident; and citizen perceptions of crowdedness at recreational facilities.**

**Measure 27. Change in perceived pleasantness of recreational experience.**

Development can affect the variety, accessibility, crowdedness, safety, and overall enjoyability of recreation in the community by adding or eliminating facilities, by changing the numbers and types of potential users, and by changing the environment around recreational facilities (by polluting the air for instance). The facilities affected may include informal open spaces such as empty lots, sidewalks, and streets used by children or adults, as well as tennis courts, swimming pools, picnic areas, gyms, playing fields, riding stables, boating areas, beaches, woodland trails, and so forth.

Even where the facilities affected by the development are private and restricted to a special group, such as pools for residents of highrises, they can affect the demand for publicly provided recreational service.[15]

### Accessibility

There are at least two ways to assess a change in access to recreation facilities. One emphasizes potential availability of facilities to all citizens, whether or not they use them. The second emphasizes the inconvenience to current users when an existing facility is to be affected. Basically the same approaches apply to evaluating past and proposed development.

Under the first approach one may identify the change in the number of persons (by age group) within (or not within) "x" distance of types of facilities to be added or removed by the new development. The "x" distance would be a criterion chosen by the community; it would be different for different types of facilities such as pools or neighborhood playgrounds. These distances can be determined from maps with travel time or distance contours around specific facilities superimposed on plots of estimated population distributions. The travel times would be computed by mode of travel (e.g., walking, car, bus), taking into account local conditions such as physical barriers.

The second approach emphasizes loss of access and may be used when a facility is eliminated by the new development or made virtually unusable because of an increased hazard, extreme environmental changes, or by construction of physical barriers to it. In this case, the **number of different people or families using the facility, the attendance rate, and the distance to the nearest equivalent facility** might be used to reflect the extent of reduced recreational opportunities.

The number of people or families using a public recreational facility can be estimated with citizen surveys, such as are starting to be used by a few recreation departments.[16] Attendance figures for the facilities do not describe the number of different users (as opposed to repeaters), but they do give a good indication of the intensity of usage by the community. For private facilities, membership rolls are usually available. Commercial recreation facilities such as bowling alleys generally keep attendance statistics.

The distance to the nearest equivalent facility is usually easy to determine, but whether that facility can handle the potential increased demand is less obvious. (See discussion of crowdedness estimates below.)

What is an acceptable distance to a substitute facility? This will vary with the age and nature of the clientele group. For example, a new development may displace an open lot—the informal play space of neighborhood children. An alternate site may be well within walking distance and a satisfactory substitute for older children, but parents who want to keep their younger children within sight and sound range may consider it unacceptable.

### Crowdedness

The impact of development on the crowding of recreational facilities may be described in terms of waiting times at facilities, number of people turned away, potential users per facility, space or facilities per resident, or usage as a percent of operating capacity (where the latter is a meaningful statistic). Citizen perceptions of crowdedness are also important to consider.

---

15. For a further discussion of recreation measures see, H.P. Hatry and D.R. Dunn, *Measuring the Effectiveness of Local Government Services: Recreation,* Washington, D.C., The Urban Institute, 1971, and *How Effective Are Your Community Recreation Services?*, U.S. Department of Interior, Bureau of Outdoor Recreation, prepared by The Urban Institute, 1973.

16. Ibid. See references listed for a discussion of utilization of citizen surveys to collect information on recreation usage and many other kinds of data.

*For evaluating past developments, actual changes in the crowdedness of facilities can be measured. Before and after waiting times can be determined from signup sheets or estimated by staff at the facilities. Observers can estimate the number of turnaways. Recorded attendance and design capacity are sometimes known and can be used to compute the percent of capacity used. And citizens can be surveyed to determine if they feel the facilities are too crowded.*

For evaluating proposed developments, rough estimates of changes in crowdedness of major facilities, such as pools and tennis courts, can be made. The specific facilities–old or new, public or private–most likely to attract people from the new development can be identified. Then the fraction of people in the new development likely to participate in each activity would be estimated according to the expected age, sex, and income distribution of the new residents, applying rates of usage for comparable people in the existing community. Accuracy of these estimates will be limited by many external factors that can affect usage, such as changes in amounts of leisure time people have, or the energy shortage. It is also affected by incomplete knowledge of how well the people will be informed about a facility's existence and how crowded, safe, and attractive they will find it–factors which appear to affect rates of usage. Accuracy is also limited by the general lack of data in many communities on usage rates for various demographic and socioeconomic groups. Some communities are just starting to identify and explain usage patterns for their existing population, however, so the prospects for better data seem to be improving.

As a poor substitute, current attendance per capita figures might be used to project expected usage and then see whether these results exceed facility capacities. The minimal and simplest approach would be to identify nearby facilities, determine which are near or at capacity (or where significant number of users already feel too crowded), and use judgment to estimate whether the new development is likely to push them over capacity, and cause more intense feelings of crowdedness.

If the new development provides additional recreation facilities, the estimated number of people who currently use other facilities and who are closer to the new ones could be subtracted from attendance figures of these current facilities to indicate the decrease in crowdedness there. This is not as simple as it may seem, since usage is affected by the available supply, and the old facility may become just as crowded as before. Also, users may not automatically switch to the more convenient facilities.

### Pleasantness

*For evaluating past developments, user surveys can estimate directly the change in the perceived pleasantness of the recreational experience before and after development, for facilities whose environment or demand is affected by the development. A second indicator could be the* **percent of previous users still in the community who continue to use the facility,** *with the assumption that an attendance loss reflects decreasing pleasantness. For example, x percent of the children using a public playground may stay away after a tougher group of children arrive. Or y percent of the previous swimmers stop using a beach because of pollution caused by a new plant. Periodic citizen surveys of use patterns and reasons for nonuse could furnish much of the necessary data.*

*A simpler but less satisfactory approach would be to consider before and after* **changes in attendance figures** *for nearby facilities, as compared to changes in attendance at facilities in areas not affected by development. This would suggest whether a facility is still considered relatively enjoyable.*

For evaluating proposed developments, a qualitative description of changes in the environment at recreation sites, and judgmental statements as to whether they are likely to affect enjoyment should be made. Quantitative projections about how citizens are likely to perceive pleasantness is beyond the current state of the art.

## EDUCATION

**Measure 28. Change in number of students within x minutes walk or y minutes ride from school, by type of school.**

**Measure 29. Number and percent of students having to switch schools or busing status (from walking to busing or vice versa).**

**Measure 30. Change in crowdedness "breakpoints" (such as need for added shifts) or indicators (such as student-teacher ratios); and student, teacher, and parent perceptions of crowdedness and pleasantness of schooling.**

New development can change the numbers, age distribution, and special educational needs of school children in the community. These can affect the location of new schools and where pupils are assigned, which in turn may affect the crowdedness, convenience, and pleasantness of the schools.

Development may also enhance the variety of educational experiences available to the community by providing the critical population mass necessary to warrant junior colleges, special classes for the educationally handicapped, experimental schools, vocational programs, and the like.

Development may affect the quality of education in the schools, but too little is known about measuring, let

*[Paragraphs in italics deal with retrospective analyses]*

alone predicting, quality changes for any recommendations to be made here on what to measure. If the current debates and research on educational quality shed more light on cause-and-effect relationships, the findings may be incorporated in new impact measures.

Effects of development on education that *can* be estimated, and that are of considerable interest in the community, are changes in the convenience, accessibility, crowdedness and pleasantness of schools. For example, how many pupils will have to switch schools? How many who walk will have to use buses and vice versa? Will severe crowding result, forcing the schools to go to a two-shift system? (It should be noted that less pronounced changes in crowdedness are difficult to measure meaningfully.) How will pupil-teacher ratios change? (One should not assume that these ratios necessarily relate to quality of education, but the data may suggest possible change in the amount of attention given to each pupil.) Will present classroom capacity serve the greater demands? (Stated capacities usually should not be taken literally but may serve as benchmarks of crowding; again, this is not a quality of education measure.) Will there be new types of educational opportunity not previously available to the community?

Data should be collected for individual schools and aggregated by level of school–elementary, junior, and high school–where appropriate.

*For evaluating past developments, data on pupil reassignments, total enrollments, design capacities, and variety of schools and programs should be readily available from the local board of education. Average travel times, if not explicitly available, can be computed from maps showing locations of schools, school jurisdictional boundaries, population or student distributions, and school busing boundaries. Surveys of students, teachers, and parents could be used to identify changes in the perceptions about the pleasantness and crowdedness of the schools before and after development. It should be noted that changes in school busing policy which modify the neighborhood school concept may overshadow effects of individual new developments.*

For evaluating proposed developments, most communities have statistics on the number of pupils expected for elementary, junior high, and secondary schools per housing unit by type of housing. (As discussed for Measure 1, these data are also needed for computing educational expenditures and the change in public fiscal flows.) Expected increases in demand, balanced against present school capacity and planned new schools, can be used to estimate pupil assignments to various schools and likely crowdedness. These estimates, in light of known busing policies, will indicate how many pupils will face changed transportation arrangements. The local board of education must be consulted, since the results of new development will be heavily influenced by their decisions about how to deal with increased demands. Qualitative, judgmental estimates of whether there will be any important changes in perceived crowdedness and pleasantness should also be made.

## LOCAL TRANSPORTATION

**Measure 31. Change in vehicular travel times between selected origins and destinations.**

**Measure 32. Change in duration and severity of congestion.**

**Measure 33. Change in likelihood of finding a satisfactory parking space within x distance from destination or residence.**

**Measure 34. Change in numbers and percent of residents with access to public transit within x feet of their residences; and numbers and percent of employees who can get within x distance of work location by public transit.**

**Measure 35. Change in the rate of traffic accidents (or expert rating of change in hazard presented).**

**Measure 36. Number and percent of citizens perceiving a change in neighborhood traffic hazard; and change in pedestrian usage of streets, sidewalks, and other outdoor space.**

Development may affect vehicular travel by changing the number and length of car trips needed, by changing local street and road patterns, by creating need for additional traffic controls, and by changing the demand and supply for parking space.

Development may affect the accessibility and convenience of public transportation by altering demand patterns, and thus routing, scheduling, and crowdedness.

Walking and bicycle riding are too infrequently given serious attention as forms of transportation. These, also, may be affected by development that adds or interferes with sidewalks, bridges, paths, and bikeways, that changes relative locations of shopping, work centers, and residences, and that alters the traffic hazards to pedestrians and bicycle riders.

Transportation impacts most directly related to new developments and likely to be of most concern to citizens include travel times, degree of congestion, parking availability, public transit accessibility, and traffic safety. Other indicators may be appropriate in particular situations. Pedestrian accessibility to recreation, schools, and shopping is reflected in Measures 25, 28 and 37, respectively. Effects on bicycle transportation should be discussed at least qualitatively where pertinent. As with other impacts, distinctions should be made between changes in transportation service for the existing community and transportation service for the new development.[17]

## Travel Times

The only noticeable effect on travel times for many developments–especially small ones–is likely to be in their immediate vicinity or on the nearby portions of roads radiating from the area of the development, which receive the full brunt of the increased traffic load. The nearby effects are also often the only ones that can be readily estimated without using detailed models of the transportation network. **Changes in average driving speeds** might be a complementary or alternative measure to travel times; especially when traffic effects on small stretches of roads in the vicinity of the development are the only ones considered, the absolute change in travel time may not adequately reflect the potential inconvenience to drivers who are forced to drive more slowly than previously.

*For past developments, increased time to get into or out of the immediate vicinity of the development and delays on major roads leading from the vicinity of the development can be measured by a sample of test runs before and after development.*

For proposed developments, the existing street capacities and traffic volumes are usually known or measurable. To this base the expected change in car trips caused by the development should be added. The number of car trips generated by each household unit can be estimated based on the type and price of unit, expected socioeconomic characteristics of the occupants, and the expected modal split between car and other means of transportation. Similar estimates can be made by type of business for industrial and commercial development. From these data local delays can be roughly estimated and likely bottlenecks identified.

For a development that is large relative to its community, or for the cumulative effects of a set of developments, the change in travel times between major origins and destinations throughout the community should be considered in addition to localized effects.

For developments in residential areas, the localized travel time effects can be assessed in terms of the change in travel time to major work or shopping destinations from the vicinity of the development. For developments in commercial and industrial areas, changes in travel time to existing business from major residential locations or other business locations can be used. For both cases, changes in travel times through the area of the development should be reported if major through-routes are affected.

Except where the road network is quite sparse, such an analysis often is difficult and expensive. It may only be feasible to collect data on travel times between points near the development and a few representative work, shopping, or residential locations as discussed above for localized travel times.

*For past developments, communitywide travel time changes can be measured by test driving along selected paths before and after development. Work trip times should be collected for a.m. and p.m. rush hours; other trip times should be tested in off-peak conditions. Locations in and around the development for use as one end of the point-to-point trips should be selected carefully because the effect of the development on travel times may vary considerably depending on the points' locations with respect to the exits and internal traffic flows of the development.*[18]

*There are many practical problems in collecting valid travel time data at two points in time, and then attempting to isolate the changes due to the development. Care must be taken that time of day, weather conditions, and the paths used are similar. Traffic changes due to changes in the base population or to other developments must be considered. Also, the traffic load imposed by a development often changes over time as its novelty wears off, as motorists find new ways to cope with it as its existence becomes known, and as its usage builds to capacity. Thus, a retrospective analysis should preferably be made for several points in time, to identify the transient effects.*

*A cruder, less reliable approach is to obtain* **subjective impressions of travel times from drivers** *who regularly drive to and from the vicinity of the development before and after development.*

For proposed developments, estimating precise changes in travel times between pairs of points is difficult. The most common general approach starts with estimating the number of vehicular trips that will be generated by the development, based on past trips per household or business and choices between public and private modes. The expected traffic volumes on various roads can be computed by making assumptions as to how the added trips will be distributed throughout the road network during rush hours and nonrush hours, and adding them to existing volumes, taking account of expected changes by current users. The

17. For a more complete discussion of measures of effectiveness for local transportation see, R.E. Winnie and H. Hatry, *Measures of Effectiveness of Local Government Services: Local Transportation*, Washington, D.C., The Urban Institute, 1972.

18. Ibid, for a further discussion of measuring congestion and travel times.

*[Paragraphs in italics deal with retrospective analyses]*

average travel speeds can then be estimated from projected traffic volumes and known street characteristics.

For more than very simple networks, a computer model is likely to be needed to make travel time estimates. The Urban Transportation Planning Process model has been in widespread use for many years. However, such models are generally expensive to use and require considerable traffic engineering expertise. They are probably not practical nor necessary for any but the largest developments or for estimating cumulative effects, especially if the analyses are to consider alternative paths drivers may choose as their prime choices become too congested. The validity of estimates made with the aid of such models is still controversial.

Since there are many assumptions involved in estimating travel times, a range of possible delays or improvements should be given along with the best estimate of the average delay or improvement. If the range is wide, that will emphasize the lack of knowledge about the likely impact of the development. The uncertainty is important to consider in the evaluation.

## Congestion

The *severity* of congestion can be defined as the ratio of the maximum time to travel between two points relative to the "no traffic" or off-peak, law-abiding travel time between those points. The *duration* of congestion can be defined as the length of time during which travel times between two points is some percentage above the off-peak travel time.

*For past developments, before and after measurements of these two aspects of congestion can be made for nearby roads, streets, or major arteries along with travel time measurements.*[19]

Assessing the impact of a proposed development on congestion requires estimating travel times for several points in time to determine the severity and duration of the congestion. This is difficult to do with sufficient precision using existing models and with the lack of accurate knowledge of trip generation. But at least a sensitivity analysis could be undertaken for larger developments to identify the potential range of impacts that may occur under different, plausible assumptions about their trip generation. As for the analysis of travel times, it is necessary to consider alternative paths that may be used as congestion increases on the primary ones.

## Parking Convenience

The effect of a development on neighborhood parking will depend on its size, the number of new parking spaces provided by the development or the local government, the nature of the activities in the development, the availability of public transportation, existing demand in the neighborhood, and the prices charged for the new parking spaces. If the spaces provided are too few or too expensive, persons in the development may park in the surrounding neighborhood, increasing parking congestion.[20]

The major parking impact to measure is the change in the likelihood of finding an "acceptable" parking space within x distance from the vicinity of a new development. This can be translated as the **probability that a parking space exists within x distance at a given time of day and within a given price range.** In some situations, the analysis might also distinguish availability of on-street and off-street parking, metered and nonmetered parking, and so forth.

An alternative or supplementary measure is the **change in the percent of people finding parking inconvenient in the vicinity of the development**, which, as with other perception measures, is more suitable for evaluating past than proposed developments. Another measure, **the number of spaces on the development site relative to the number needed to serve the development** can indicate the potential for parking spillover into the neighborhood, but its effect on neighborhood parking depends on the existing parking conditions. Yet another measure, **the average percent of available neighborhood parking spaces that are filled** at various times of day and days of week, is a weak measure of parking adequacy, because of the ambiguity in interpreting it; a low level may indicate sufficiency or undesirability of the parking. A high level—close to 100 percent—may indicate just the right amount or a shortage. The interpretation can be improved by considering the percentage filled by price range, and other attributes of the parking spaces.

*For past developments, the before and after change in parking availability can be determined by observation, test, or survey. Aerial photos of the neighborhood could be used in some situations to identify the number of empty parking spaces relative to the total number of available legal spaces at an instant of time. The turnover will not be identifiable unless a series of photos is used. (The photos would not be suitable, of course, in situations where there is a lot of underground or covered parking.)*

For proposed development, the measures might be roughly estimated from the expected shortage or excess of parking spaces available in the proposed development for its own needs, and the number of spaces typically available in the adjacent neighborhood (during business and nonbusiness hours). The latter can be measured by field observations or aerial photos. The estimate can be crudely

19. Ibid.

20. Parking lots and parking spillovers to the neighborhood are factors to consider in the attractiveness Measures 14 and 15.

based on the average deficit (or surplus) of spaces expected in the neighborhood after development, or on a mathematical model that could be developed for translating changes in parking supply and demand into the expected time to find a space.

### Accessibility to Public Transportation

New development may generate enough demand to allow additional service on existing public transit lines, the creation or rerouting of lines, or even the start of a new public transit system. If so, estimates should be made of the change in the number and percent of existing residents within y distance of service from their residences. Distances of one-eighth or one-quarter of a mile—roughly a 5 or 10 minute walk—might be used as standards. More detailed measures that indicate the time it takes to get to representative destinations via public transit may be appropriate for some situations.

Whether transit service gets changed or not, it may still be of interest to the community to see whether the new development will add to or reduce the community's dependence on autos.[21] This can be measured by **the percent of new residents who will be within y distance of public transit, and the percent who could reasonably get to work by public transit** (not that they necessarily will use it). Time limits and walking distances that would define a "reasonable" work trip can be defined according to local tastes. For commercial and industrial development, the measure is **the percent of workers and customers who can get to the development by public transit.**

Changes in accessibility of public transportation for people living near or in a development can be estimated using maps showing local transit stops and the number of people living within x miles of the stops. The same procedure applies for past and proposed developments.

The accessibility of a commercial or industrial development for its employees or visitors can be estimated for past development by surveying them, or, for past and proposed developments by estimating whether areas from which customers or employees are likely to come are partially or wholly accessible by public transit. Planned (or proposed) changes in routes as a result of the development should be considered.

21. Dependence on autos may be important for more than just air pollution impacts, which are covered in Measure 5. Some communities have the goal "to increase the percent of residents who can reasonably get to work by public transit." Of course the people who will reside or work in the new development will be interested in their accessibility to public transit too, but that is not the motivation behind this measurement.

### Traffic Hazards

Increased or decreased traffic hazards in the neighborhood of the development, especially hazards to pedestrians and children, should be a major concern in impact evaluations. Both the actual hazard and the hazard perceived by the citizens are important; the latter may have the greater impact on behavior.

Changes in accident rates (per thousand people) caused by increased traffic and special hazards created or eliminated by development will partly indicate changes in the actual hazard. However, even for past developments, it may prove too difficult to estimate the change in the accident rate for *existing residents*, or to relate observed changes in the accident rate to a specific development, even with detailed evaluation studies. In those cases, a proxy measure, **the change in the traffic hazard presented to residents of the neighborhood**, might suffice. It would be based on expert opinion of how changes in street and parking layouts, traffic density, view obstruction, and traffic controls combine to change the hazard. If the change in hazard cannot be expressed as a quantitative estimate of the change in the accident rate, then a scale describing whether the danger is "much greater, somewhat greater, about the same, somewhat less, or much less" should be used.

A sharp increase in actual or perceived traffic hazard may curtail street and sidewalk usage by pedestrians, children playing, and other outdoor activities. This reduction in activity may limit or even reduce the number of accidents. Thus it is desirable to include an expert hazard rating even where it is possible to measure or estimate changes in accident rates.

The hazard perceived by the community can be described in terms of changes in activities that are considered safe. These may range from "sidewalks or streets usable for young children at play" at the safe end of the scale to "not suitable for an adult walking" at the other, unsafe end of the scale.

*In estimating the impact of past developments on traffic safety, data on reported accidents are available from local police agencies, and usually include the location of the accident. From these data can be sorted incidents that occur on streets near the development. As mentioned earlier, however, attributing the causes to a particular development is often difficult, unless an obvious hazard exists. Expert opinion of traffic engineers and police can be used to rate the changes in hazard before and after development. Perceived traffic hazards can be estimated by before and after surveys of parents and children in the neighborhood.*

Hazard rating of streets in the neighborhood of a proposed development can again be made by traffic engineers and police based on expected changes in traffic volumes, types of traffic (such as trucks), signals or signs, sightlines, and other factors. Neighborhood perceptions of the current hazard may be collected by citizen surveys as a baseline for estimating possible changes. If citizens feel very safe today when there is low traffic and the likely volume will increase sharply, educated guesses as to changes in perceptions can be made. It is probably not reliable to use the survey to elicit citizens opinions on what their perceptions will be after development, except perhaps when extreme changes in conditions are expected.

## SHOPPING

**Measure 37. Change in the number of stores and services, by type, available within x distance of y people.**

**Measure 38. Change in the percent of people generally satisfied with local shopping conditions (access, variety, crowdedness).**

Commercial developments may increase the number and types of retail stores and alter the community's access to shopping opportunities. Residential growth may crowd existing stores with new customers and displace some stores–though commercial facilities often expand to meet additional demand.

Most people want access to a variety of types of stores, and a choice among stores of a given type. Stores also serve as casual meeting places and for other social purposes as well as for providing goods.[22]

The suggested measures deal with accessibility and overall citizen satisfaction with local shopping as affected by development. These measures are intended primarily for residential neighborhoods but may be applied to shopping conditions near work centers for the lunchtime and after-workday buyers.

### Accessibility

Data on accessibility should be collected to show the approximate change in the number of people who can get to major types of stores or shopping centers within 5 to 15 minutes walking (one-eighth to one-half miles), within an x-minute car ride or within a y-minute public transit ride.

These data, for both past and proposed developments, can be estimated by plotting store locations and population distributions before and after development on a map, and using knowledge of local walking, driving, or public transportation travel times. Large department stores and chain stores often obtain such information and might make it available. Of course, everyone does not patronize the nearest stores, but assuming that most people do will suffice for most impact analysis purposes.

### Citizen Satisfaction

Perceptions of the overall adequacy of local shopping facilities can be collected by citizen surveys in the neighborhood of the development (preferably as part of citizen surveys required for other measures). Overall perceptions will be difficult to project for proposed development. However, perceptions of the overall satisfaction with existing shopping could be used as a basis for making qualitative estimates of how expected changes in shopping might affect the neighborhood. For example, if residents consider shopping in current stores satisfactory, a proposed new supermarket requiring rezoning might have less merit than if current citizen perceptions were that shopping conditions were completely adequate.

22. For a general discussion of the role business establishments play in the social life of urban neighborhoods, see J. Jacobs, *The Death and Life of Great American Cities*, New York, Random House, 1969.

# V. HOUSING AND SOCIAL CONDITIONS

Somewhat surprisingly, the impact of new residential development on community housing needs is not always considered in evaluating proposed developments. Often this is because of the false assumption that natural market actions balance supply and demand. The private housing market frequently fails as a provider of housing needs, especially for families in the lower income ranges. Impact analyses should attempt to assess changes in the housing supply, in terms of community housing needs. However, housing should not be viewed, in assessing impact, only in terms of new or existing physical structures. Viewed more broadly, housing involves meeting certain needs and preferences for a large range of services. In this context, housing is seen as a delivery system for these services.

The effects of new housing on the price of existing housing, and the impact on prices if new residential development is constrained, should both also be considered. Such price changes affect the ability of households to obtain adequate housing or, if renting, even to stay in the community. Techniques for estimating prices change effects are still under development.

But the area probably given least attention in most evaluations is the impact of a development on neighborhood social conditions–the interaction of people with one another, the ways in which residents (and workers) use the neighborhood, and their attitudes or perception of the neighborhood as a place to live or work.

The impact on social conditions should be assessed by considering the changes to a series of interrelated factors:

- Displacement and relocation of existing residents and workers.
- Social interaction patterns and their perceived importance (by local residents and workers).
- Outdoor activity patterns (such as playing, sitting, walking and socializing) and their perceived importance.
- Pedestrian accessibility to shopping, recreation, and schools.
- Perceptions of neighborhood traffic hazards.
- Feeling of security from crime.
- Attitudes toward neighborhood–such as attractiveness, friendliness, crowdedness, and overall desirableness as a place to live or work.

Some aspects of these factors have been discussed in sections on recreation, education, shopping, transportation and aesthetics. This section emphasizes those considerations not previously discussed. But they all should be considered together to better understand likely neighborhood impacts.

It is difficult to predict how these social conditions may change over time. The state of the art is such that one can at most be confident in describing how people *presently* use and perceive of their neighborhood. By conducting before and after (retrospective) case studies of the impacts of developments on their neighborhoods and comparative studies of "control" neighborhoods similar in terms of socioeconomic and demographic characteristic of residents and physical design aspects of housing structure or layout, one can begin to develop a basis for estimating changes in users' behaviors and attitudes likely to be brought about by development. That is, given current status of a neighborhood and a repertory of case studies, one might be able to make improved estimates of changes likely to occur in neighborhood social conditions. Despite the difficulty in doing these types of studies, these social issues are often at the heart of neighborhood concerns regarding proposed developments, and they should be explicitly considered.

These suggestions for measuring impacts on housing and social conditions are offered because these areas are so crucial. But it is underscored that many of the measurement procedures discussed here for these areas represent preliminary approaches that remain to be tested.

## HOUSING ADEQUACY

**Measure 39. Change in number and percent of housing units that are substandard, and change in number and percent of people living in such units.**

**Measure 40. Change in number and percent of housing units by type (price or rent range, zoning category, owner-occupied and rental, etc.) relative to demand or to number of families in various income classes in the community.**

Residential development obviously affects the housing stock in the community by providing new housing units. Development of any kind may also change the housing stock by destroying existing housing on the site. Commercial and industrial developments may affect housing indirectly by their effect on jobs and the local economy, which in turn may alter housing demand, prices, rates of abandonment, upkeep, and crowding.

Housing objectives differ in many communities. Some that have undergone rapid recent growth are attempting to slow or stop new housing. Others, attempting to cash in on growth, are promoting primary or vacation residences. Still others are attempting to improve housing for low- and middle-income families, and some central cities are making a special bid to attract the affluent

Because of this diversity, communities must devise their own sets of housing measures. The recommended measures simply aim to describe some fairly universal concerns–effects of new development on substandard housing, changes in the mix of housing, and impact on housing needs of existing residents. A community could then convert these raw data into measures more closely attuned to their desired housing mix or desired direction of change. Preferably, proposed changes in housing would be related quantitatively to community housing mix needs and objectives. If this is too complex in some circumstances, an alternative approach is to make ad hoc judgments on whether the new mix is desirable.

### Changes in Substandard Housing

A goal of most communities is the elimination of substandard housing. Measure 39 indicates the absolute and percentage changes in substandard units and in people living in them. "Substandard" must be defined explicitly in each community. The criteria may be serious violations of building or health codes or U.S. Census terminology ("dilapidated or deteriorated" as defined in the 1960 Census, or incomplete plumbing, as defined in 1970). Data on the number of substandard units to be removed and the totals remaining in the community are often known. If the community has not kept independent records, the count of substandard housing in the 1970 Census can be used as a base. This inventory can be updated from cumulative records of units razed, from sample data provided by building, fire, and health inspectors, and from general knowledge of community conditions by welfare officials and others.

Note that adding new housing units will automatically reduce the *percentage* of total units that are substandard and the *percentage* of citizens living in them without necessarily alleviating the existing problem at all. Therefore, the changes in absolute numbers as well as the percentages are needed.

### Changes in Housing Mix

The description of housing stock mix should be categorized by price, type, and ownership.

*Price* should be classified according to five to ten sales price or annual rent level bands. Houses and condominium apartments should be stated separately from rental units. All should be specified by number of bedrooms (efficiency, 1, 2, 3, or more).

*Type* of housing should distinguish among single-family detached, townhouse, garden apartment, and high-rise. Consideration should be given to using finer distinctions such as lot size, and multifamily dwellings by number of apartment units contained.

*Ownership* classifies dwellings as rented or owner-occupied. Many believe that there is some relationship between ownership status and upkeep, neighborhood stability, and community participation.

It often may be desirable to present these categories of the housing mix by different areas or neighborhoods of the jurisdiction.

The above measures can best be used to describe the *instantaneous* change in substandard housing and the variety of housing available after a particular development occurs. The *ultimate* effect on the housing stock is more complex and is a function of the percent of new residents that transfer from within the community; whether the new residents are newly created family units; who (if anyone) fills their vacated residences, and so on down the price chain. What happens at the end of this chain–e.g., an abandoned unit, a unit sharply decreased in value, a stable low-priced home–will determine the long-range changes in the housing mix and total housing stock in the community. It may take some time for this chain to work itself out.[1]

For past and proposed developments, data on the number and type of units added or torn down by the development are almost always available. These can be added to the housing mix data before construction to determining the immediate changes. Most of the desired baseline data need only be approximate to give an adequate idea of how the development will influence the major characteristics of the mix. Housing price data can be based on current sales prices from information collected by realtors. In the absence of such data, assessment records can be used, adjusting the data by the use of assessed-to-market-value ratios based on state or federal studies available for larger communities and counties. Planning departments usually have data on the number of housing units by type or zoning category. Market research studies by area realtors and businesses are other potential sources of data on housing prices, types, and styles. Ownership status can be determined from sampling property tax records.

### Estimating Housing Needs

At present, there does not seem to be any completely satisfactory approach to identifying community housing needs quantitatively. Several interim approaches may be considered while awaiting development of better methods still in research.

One means of estimating housing need is to relate the current costs of housing and local income distribution patterns to some norm. For example, the average American family, based on Department of Labor statistics, allocates 17 to 22 percent of income to housing, varying by ownership status and income level. The degree to which a community has a reasonable match between rent levels, home values and income provides a rough reflection of how well supply meets need. The 1970 Census provides data on the proportion of owner-occupied units by value and the proportion of rental units by monthly rents. These would have to be sharply adjusted for cost-of-living changes since then.[2]

However, there are many problems with simply linking housing need to income. Households of similar income but different demographic characteristics do not have the same needs. For example, persons over 65 represent a high proportion of those who pay a higher-than-average share of *current income* for housing because savings and household size play a major role in determining what housing people can afford. College students, with little or no income, also represent a special case. Thus it would be more realistic to develop different income-to-housing-price norms for at least different age groups and different household sizes.

HUD FHA demand estimates from the "Analysis of Housing Market" series present further guidance about estimated housing demand by price range and county in metropolitan areas.[3] The statistics are based on existing intracommunity income characteristics rather than housing needs of inmigrants. For example, only 6 percent of the housing demand in one affluent county is for units under $30,000, while an adjacent county is cited as needing 31 percent of its units in this price range.[4] These reports, issued for large SMSA's primarily to identify housing needs for lower income groups, also provide estimates of demand for rental units by rent level and number of bedrooms.

Further insight into housing needs may be obtained by determining **occupancy rates** for various types and prices of standard housing. Low occupancy rates for a particular type—assuming the features and neighborhood are acceptable—would raise questions if more housing of this type were proposed. High occupancy rates, say above 95 percent, might suggest that more stock may be needed to meet demand or to at least make the market more fluid. Note that low occupancy rates may be due to undesirable features of the unoccupied housing or its neighborhood, and not because demand is being satisfied.

Areawide housing market models, such as one currently under development by deLeeuw,[5] should make it possible to improve estimates of housing demand and the effect of development on demand, but these models are still in the research stage.

## PEOPLE DISPLACED

**Measure 41. Number of residents or workers displaced by development—and whether they are satisfied with having to move.**

Development may uproot current residents by physically displacing their homes. Less obviously, development may cause people to move because of its effect on taxes or on the physical or social environment.

1. A discussion of the housing chain as it affects the poor may be found in John B. Lansing, Charles Wade Clifton, and James N. Morgan, *New Homes and Poor People, A Study of Chains of Moves*, Survey Research Center, Institute for Social Research, University of Michigan, Maxwell Printing, 1969.

2. Related issues, not further discussed in this paper, are the effects that new construction, or constraints placed on new development, have on the cost of housing.

3. For example, Department of Housing and Urban Development, *Analysis of the Washington, D.C., Housing Market*, Washington, D.C., 1972.

4. Ibid, Department of Housing and Urban Development.

5. Frank deLeeuw, Raymond Struyk, Sue Marshall, *Urban Institute Housing Model: Second Year Report*, Washington, D.C., The Urban Institute, 1973.

Development can also displace workers by removing existing stores and other enterprises. When certain jobs are eliminated and not moved to a convenient new location or substituted for by new jobs in the development, the net loss of employment could cause some people to leave the jurisdiction entirely.

At a minimum, the number of residents and workers who will be displaced by a development should be reported. Preferably, data should show whether those displaced are satisfied with the prospect of moving, whether they are to be compensated, how many may be given temporary quarters (and for how long), the percent expected to return to improved conditions as a result of the development, and the number of people leaving the community after development (and their reasons for so doing).

*For past developments, the number of people directly displaced can be estimated from a knowledge of the housing or commercial units torn down and their occupancy rates, if not known precisely. Census and other data on the number of occupants per unit may be used. Those displaced can be surveyed to see if they left willingly, and a sample of people who chose to leave the adjacent neighborhood can be surveyed to determine if the cause was development related.*

For proposed developments, basically the same procedure applies, except that surveys of people planning to leave the neighborhood (apart from those displaced) would be difficult to carry out and interpret. Instead, possible changes in property taxes (which can be estimated from fiscal data discussed earlier) could be used to determine the increase in housing costs–at least the tax portion for people in different house price ranges. Making simple assumptions about family incomes for different house price ranges, and using simple rules of thumb, such as no more than 25 percent of income should be spent on housing, a rough estimate of the number of families near or over the borderline can be made. This will indicate the approximate number of families who can no longer afford to live in the community. Of course, the sacrifice people may wish to make to stay, the cost of moving, and a host of other factors will determine whether people actually do move. The percent of people who will leave for social or physical environmental reasons may be crudely and cautiously estimated from past case histories of similar physical and socioeconomical changes in neighborhoods.

## POPULATION MIX

**Measure 42. Change in the population distribution by age, income, religion, racial or ethnic group, occupational class, and household type.**

Some communities may wish to encourage a diversity of people within the community. Some may prefer not to have any explicit policy other than equal opportunity. If a policy exists, individual attitudes or neighborhood objectives may differ drastically from it. One way or another, most people care about how development will affect the population mix in their neighborhood as well as at the community level.

*For past development, the census provides most of the data needed to identify the people mix in the community and in particular neighborhoods (though the latter neighborhood estimates especially may have to be updated because they can change sharply over a few years.) A survey of neighborhood residents and workers could be used to identify socioeconomic and demographic characteristics of the households and work force both before and after the development in the neighborhood and nearby areas.[6] Further estimates of the population mix may be obtained from data provided by local schools, churches, ethnic association, and realtors. Changes in the people mix due to development should be distinguished from general changes due to population shifts that are occurring in the city, metropolitan area, region, and nation.*

For proposed developments, estimates of changes in the people mix can be based on expected characteristics of the people likely to buy or rent at various price ranges, coupled with a detailed knowledge of community housing conditions, preferences, and trends. (These estimates are also needed for developing fiscal impact, recreation, education and other measures.)

## CROWDEDNESS

**Measure 43. Change in the percent of people who perceive their neighborhood as too crowded.**

Some aspects of crowdedness are reflected in the measures for transportation, recreation, education, and shopping, and in the capacity measures discussed in Part 1, Chapter I, and illustrated in Exhibit 5.

**Population density** is often used in planning and zoning matters as a measure of crowdedness. If density is used as a measure, attention should be paid not only to residential density but also to the density at various times of day and days of week. However, even at a given high

6. This survey could be the background data collected as part of a more general survey that would seek to identify citizen perceptions of privacy, crowdedness, friendliness, and other neighborhood conditions as part of other measures that have been suggested elsewhere in this report.

*[Paragraphs in italics deal with retrospective analyses]*

density, the likelihood that people will feel crowded may vary a great deal depending on the arrangement of space, the adequacy of services, and personal living styles.

Therefore, in addition to raw population densities, a direct measure of individuals' overall perceptions of community crowdedness is desirable to capture impressions that may not be adequately reflected by any of the above measures. Surveys to determine perceptions may also probe specific elements of crowding that may be especially annoying, such as too many people on the streets, traffic jams, crowding at local informal or formal recreational centers, and so forth. Information on the number of persons per room and in the building of each household surveyed should be collected to help indicate if the perceived crowding reflects primarily the crowdedness of a person's residence, of streets and service facilities, or both. (The questions on crowdedness could be part of a survey to collect data for the various perception measures suggested throughout this report.)

The expected perception of crowdedness by the community surrounding a proposed development might eventually be estimated from correlations of past surveys with estimates of the change in population density, waiting times in local facilities, percent of capacity of local facilities, neighborhood open space, increased traffic volumes, and other elements, but this is beyond the current state of the art. At present, qualitative estimates based on judgment of the effects of changes in these contributing elements of crowdedness, and by analogy with past cases, will have to suffice.

## SOCIABILITY/FRIENDLINESS

**Measure 44. Change in frequency of visits to friends among people in the existing neighborhood, and frequency of visits between people in the existing neighborhood and the new development.**

**Measure 45. Change in percent of people perceiving their neighborhood as friendly.**

While certain individuals and families seem to prefer living anonymously and in isolation, at least from the people in their immediate neighborhood, many people consider it important to live in a community where they can establish and maintain friendships. Some people also prefer a community that is generally characterized as being friendly and warm.

Development may affect both of these aspects of sociability by changing the physical proximity of people, the ease of movement (by creating or removing physical barriers such as fences, buildings, and traffic hazards) and the socioeconomic homogeneity of the neighborhood.[7]

### Data Collection for Past Development

*The degree to which new development affected the sociability or friendliness of a neighborhood may be measured by the changes in (a) the frequency of visits among people in the vicinity of a development; (b) the number of friendships and frequency of visits between people in the existing neighborhood and the new development; and (c) the percent of people perceiving changes in the degree of friendliness.*

*Measure (a) reflects the degree to which people in the vicinity of the development–but not in it or uprooted by it–have their friendships affected by the development. For a given person, the change in frequency of visiting would be expressed in terms of number of visits per month with friends within a given distance of the development (e.g., a 10-minute walk). Friends who are no longer visited because of displacement would be noted. Visiting which is continued using a change in travel modes (driving instead of walking) would still be counted as visits. Reasons for observed changes in sociability should be noted to estimate the degree to which they are affected by development-related changes in travel convenience or intangibles such as neighborhood ambience, as opposed to strictly personal reasons.*

*Measure (b) reflects the degree to which the new development is socially integrated into the neighborhood, and the degree to which new friendships may replace old friendships.*

*Measure (c) would reflect citizen perception of factors such as the ease of making friends, the amiability in stranger-to-stranger contacts, and the number of people known by sight. This is complementary to the perception of privacy, crowdedness, and overall neighborhood rating sought in other measures.*

*The main tool for collecting data for all these measurements could be a survey of citizens in the neighborhood of the development before and after development.*[8] *Direct observations of how, when and where people socialize outdoors are also important to supplement the survey data.*

---

7. For further discussion of factors influencing sociability, see A.L. Schorr, "Housing and Its Effects," in H.M. Proshansky, W.H. Ittelson, and L.G. Rivlin, eds., *Environmental Psychology*, New York, Holt, Rinehart and Winston, 1970, pp. 319-33.

8. For some sample questions that might be used in a sociability survey, and an effective format for presenting the results, see D. Appleyard and M. Lintell, "The Environmental Quality of City Streets: The Resident's Viewpoint," *American Institute of Planners Journal*, March 1972, pp. 84-101.

### Data Collection for Proposed Development

Quantitative estimates of changes in sociability as a result of a proposed development are not likely to be reliable, given the present state of knowledge. Probably the best that can be done is to make qualitative estimates of the likely direction and degree of change based on analogies to comparable past examples within the community or similar communities, and on expected changes in factors such as physical barriers, the size of the development, the number of people to be uprooted, the likely homogeneity between the existing and new socioeconomic distributions, and whether the neighborhood of the development is to be peopled with transient or long-term residents. As a base from which to make judgments, citizen surveys and direct observations can be used to estimate the current pre-development sociability in the neighborhood.

## PRIVACY

### Measure 46. Number and percent of people with change in "visual" or "auditory" privacy.

### Measure 47. Number and percent of people perceiving a loss in privacy.

Developments may affect "visual" privacy by providing new sightlines into peoples' backyards and windows and they may affect "auditory" privacy by placing additional people within earshot. They may also increase privacy by providing visual or sound screenings where none existed. A big factor may be changes in the amount of pedestrian or vehicular traffic past residences. Privacy may also be increased or decreased by more subtle changes such as the life styles of people who join the community.

Visual privacy can often be restored by defensive mechanisms such as pulling shades, building fences, and adding shrubbery, though the sense of privacy loss may remain. Auditory privacy is more difficult to remedy, though barriers or soundproofing may help.

Both objective measures of changes in sightlines and physical arrangements that affect how easy it is to hear or see personal activities, and subjective measures of peoples' perceptions of their change in privacy can be used.

In collecting objective data on loss of privacy, distinctions should be made between major intrusions, such as the first new building that lets other people look into the windows, yard, or the roof garden of an existing building, and minor intrusions which are not the first of a kind.

*Evaluation of the impact on privacy of a past development can be based on visits to the development and knowledge of the sightlines from previous buildings on the development site, using maps, plans, or photos of the area. Changes in pedestrian traffic before and after development are readily measurable. A survey of citizen perceptions of loss in privacy before and after development would take into account elements such as whether people are minding their own business as well as physical changes that affect privacy.*

Sightlines for a proposed development can be determined from plans, photos, and maps of the area. Pedestrian traffic past various residences can be estimated from the number of people who will be added to the neighborhood and their likely walking destinations. The overall impact of citizens' perceptions of privacy can probably best be estimated from experience with roughly comparable past situations. As with other measures of perceptions, a good starting point is to identify the current neighborhood perception of privacy, which then bounds the changes that are possible.

## OVERALL CONTENTMENT WITH NEIGHBORHOOD

### Measure 48. Change in percent of people who perceive their community as a good place to live.

The overall impact of a development on how people regard their community can be reflected by various direct and indirect measures. Data should be collected on the extent to which residents perceive the community as a good place to live and on **changes in lengths of residency**.[9]

Direct surveys are one of the better devices for determining how people feel about their neighborhood. The maintenance level of private homes and lawns and the types of social behavior exhibited in public may yield some further insights. Interpreting such indirect observations or measures poses serious problems, so they probably should not be used alone.

*For retrospective analyses, surveys may be taken before and after development. Probing questions will be necessary to seek reasons that people are satisfied or dissatisfied and to determine if changes during the time period are probably related to the development.*

Determining the impact of a proposed development on resident satisfaction can only be estimated by judgment based on past case histories and knowledge of the neighborhood until much more is known on how development affects the total environment, and how people's overall attitudes are affected by changes in the various elements. Surveys and regard to concerns expressed by citizens at hearings about development can help officials understand what people currently like or dislike about their neighborhoods and about growth patterns. These insights can then help form a basis for judgmental estimates about future satisfaction or discontent.

9. An attempt should be made to distinguish between changes in residency resulting from increases in housing costs or employment shifts and those resulting more directly from the development in question.

# APPENDIX

## OTHER IMPACT MEASURES CONSIDERED

In addition to the measures presented in Exhibit 1, a number of others were considered but deemed less suitable for immediate widespread use for a variety of reasons, such as their apparent lesser importance or their data collection difficulties.

Some of these other measures are presented in Exhibit 7 and are discussed in the following pages. For certain communities, some of these may be as important as those in the main body. Matters concerning the microclimate around tall buildings are considered especially important in the San Francisco area, for example. Also, to mention briefly some alternative issues underscores the earlier point that community judgments of what is important locally should influence the compilation of the list of measures to be used.

### Financial Stability of Developer

In approving developments, the fiscal soundness of the developer should be considered, perhaps as part of the preliminary review of a developer's initial application. If a builder goes bankrupt during the construction phase, structures can remain incomplete and become eyesores during the period of litigation. The jurisdiction may incur expenses, such as the provision of roads and sewers, but fail to receive anticipated payment from the builder or residents. And the potential residents of the development may lose some or all of their investment.

### Change in Personal Income Per Household

Interesting as this information would be, the impact of an individual development on income for most existing households is likely to be small and difficult to estimate. Incomes of new persons in the new development can be estimated, but the primary and secondary effects of their spending on other people's incomes require many assumptions and are unlikely to result in reliable or useful findings. For commercial development the most direct effect will be through jobs and will be indirectly reflected by the employment measures (2-3) in Exhibit 1.

### Change in Utility Costs

Telephone, electric, gas, and water utility rates may be subject to economies or diseconomies of scale. Costs to the consumer may, therefore, change as a function of development. In addition, developments that are remote or cause special service problems may lead to the shifting of these additional utility costs to all residents instead of higher costs for just those enjoying the benefits. Data may be obtainable from utility companies in some cases, but cost attribution is complex.

### Change in Available Agricultural and Commercial Forest Land

Although changes in agricultural lands are more often concerns at regional or state levels, some local governments may also wish to keep track of how their agricultural and forest resources are affected by the encroachments of development, especially where such special purpose or prime land is a central feature of the local economy.

### Change in Microclimate

The sunshine, wind, and temperature of a street can be affected by the development along it. Rows of tall buildings lining a street affect sun exposure and create a canyon effect that may drastically change winds and air pollution conditions.

### Land Pollution

In some communities such as New York City, dog excrement has become a problem on sidewalks and in playgrounds and parks. In Washington, D.C., the lead content of inner-city soil has increased due to traffic and is thought to be a health hazard because of its ingestion by

*EXHIBIT 7*

**OTHER IMPACT MEASURES CONSIDERED**

| Impact Area | Measure |
| --- | --- |
| *Local Economy* | Financial stability of developer. |
| | Change in personal income per household. |
| | Change in utility costs. |
| *Natural Environment* | Change in available agricultural or commercial forest land. |
| | Change in microclimate. |
| | Land pollution. |
| *Services* | Storm drainage quality. |
| | Additional measures of changes in the quality of local government services. |
| *Health and Safety* | Changes in death and illness rates. |
| | Level of hazard to workers and public during construction. |
| | Level of structural safety. |
| *Local Transportation* | Change in car trips or car miles per person per day. |
| *Social Conditions* | Consumer protection measures. |
| | Neighborhood stability–change in tenure rates. |

children. Developments can have an impact on these problems as well as more traditional soil problems such as salinity, chemical imbalance, erosion, and pollution of ground water.

### Storm Drainage Quality

Extremely poor storm drainage in a development will affect the frequency of flooding and is, therefore, dealt with in Measure 12 of Exhibit 1. However, less drastic effects of inadequate storm drainage—such as minor flooding of streets, gutters, and lawns—still have nuisance and negative aesthetic value and may also be considered. Many building codes provide drainage controls, but where these codes are lacking, a special measure may be useful, especially for protecting areas adjacent to new development.

### Additional Measures of Changes in the Quality of Local Government Services

Development may affect solid waste collection, street cleanliness, and other public services besides those reflected in the main list. Whenever it appears that a new development might impair the quality of local government services not covered by the main list of impact measures, appropriate additional measures should be added to the list.

### Changes in Death and Illness Rates

New developments can affect community health by their impacts on pollution, housing, sanitation, and drinking water conditions; by the health, hygiene, and age distribution of the people they attract; and by their influence on psychological stresses. The synergistic effects of these elements on death and illness rates are important but are not feasible to estimate with current knowledge.

### Level of Hazard to Workers and Public During Construction

Construction safety is regulated by many local codes, but the likelihood of any hazards other than the usual ones would merit special attention.

### Level of Structural Safety

The assumption behind the measures in Exhibit 1 is that building codes adequately provide for monitoring the structural safety and suitability of the soil for most developments. Where the codes do not exist or are inadequate, the safety features would be an important measure in the evaluation.

### Change in Car Trips or Car Miles Per Person Per Day

This measure might be considered an indicator of how the development affects people's dependence on cars. A growing number of people wish to reduce their dependence on cars, something that many planners have long felt would make for better cities. Even the "cleaner" cars now being engineered will still create problems of congestion, safety, and energy consumption. The measure might be applied to (a) people in the development, considering their average miles per day before and after living in the development, and (b) people in the community, especially where a commercial or industrial development affects work and shopping proximity to residences. It might be especially useful to determine the trend in dependence on cars over time.

### Consumer Protection Measures

Measures in Exhibit 1 do not include the amenities or quality that the buyer or renter of a development gets for his money, though some important aspects of consumer protection, however, are included in measures dealing with health and safety, crime, fire, natural disaster, drinking water, and pollution. It might also be pertinent in evaluating whether a development should proceed to check the developer's record for fair dealing. A particularly bad record in this respect might be grounds for disallowing further development by him in the community.

### Neighborhood Stability—Change in Tenure Rates

Preserving the stability of a neighborhood is an oft-expressed objective of residents. It usually implies a desire to have people around long enough to have lasting friendships or many acquaintances, or to have people in the community who will care about it and maintain it. However, sheer length of tenure is not an end in itself and many factors in society outside the neighborhood or community encourage mobility. It is believed that measures in Exhibit 1 dealing with satisfaction with the community will come close to telling most communities what they need to know about stability.